A SHORT PHILOSOPHICAL GUIDE TO THE FALLACIES OF LOVE

A SHORT PHILOSOPHICAL GUIDE TO THE FALLACIES OF LOVE

JOSÉ A. DÍEZ
and
ANDREA IACONA

BLOOMSBURY ACADEMIC
LONDON • NEW YORK • OXFORD • NEW DELHI • SYDNEY

BLOOMSBURY ACADEMIC
Bloomsbury Publishing Plc
50 Bedford Square, London, WC1B 3DP, UK
1385 Broadway, New York, NY 10018, USA

BLOOMSBURY, BLOOMSBURY ACADEMIC and the Diana logo are trademarks of
Bloomsbury Publishing Plc

First published in Great Britain 2021

Cover design by Louise Dugdale
Cover image: Castello di Masino (Turin, Italy).
Photograph by Karla Camila Harada.

A catalogue record for this book is available from the British Library.

Library of Congress Cataloging-in-Publication Data
Names: Díez, José A., 1961– author. | Iacona, Andrea, author.
Title: A short philosophical guide to the fallacies of love /
José A. Díez and Andrea Iacona.
Description: London ; New York : Bloomsbury Academic, 2020. |
Includes bibliographical references and index.
Identifiers: LCCN 2020033586 (print) | LCCN 2020033587 (ebook) |
ISBN 9781350140905 (hb) | ISBN 9781350140899 (pb) |
ISBN 9781350140882 (epdf) | ISBN 9781350140875 (ebook)
Subjects: LCSH: Love. Classification: LCC BD436 .D485 2020 (print) |
LCC BD436 (ebook) | DDC 128/.46–dc23
LC record available at https://lccn.loc.gov/2020033586
LC ebook record available at https://lccn.loc.gov/2020033587

ISBN: HB: 978-1-3501-4090-5
PB: 978-1-3501-4089-9
ePDF: 978-1-3501-4088-2
eBook: 978-1-3501-4087-5

Typeset by Newgen KnowledgeWorks Pvt. Ltd., Chennai, India

To find out more about our authors and books visit www.bloomsbury.com
and sign up for our newsletters.

To those who deceive themselves
(That is, to everybody)
To Camila

CONTENTS

PREFACE

This book was initially conceived as an English version of *Del amor y otros engaños* (Alphadecay, 2016), which in turn is a free Spanish translation of *Amore e altri inganni* (Indiana, 2104). But we have changed the Spanish text substantially, rewriting entire parts of it and adding new material. So we no longer know whether the final result may still be regarded as an extremely free translation of *Amore e altri inganni* or is simply another book. No matter how you want to call it, however, we hope that we have made some progress in improving the original.

Since we have been thinking about the issues discussed in this book for a long time, we owe thanks to lots of people for helping us think through them and shape our ideas. These people include friends, colleagues, anonymous referees or simply persons who decided to spend a couple of hours listening to us. If you are one of them, please forgive us for not knowing or remembering your name.

We would like to thank Darlhen Louis, Vikram Mukhija and Zsofia Zvolenszky for their thoughtful reading of a previous version of the text. Their comments were really helpful. We are also grateful to Bernardino Sassoli for facilitating the process of publishing in English. Finally, we owe much to Kevin Mulligan and Richard Davies for their interest in our project, for their invaluable support and for the innumerable corrections and suggestions they provided. From them we have learned a lot about English, literature and philosophy.

ACKNOWLEDGEMENTS

The translations from Italian and Spanish provided in the endnotes are by Richard Davies, José Díez and Andrea Iacona. Every effort has been made to trace copyright holders and to obtain their permission for the use of copyright material. We apologize for any errors or omissions and would be grateful if notified of any corrections that should be incorporated in future reprints or editions of this book.

Introduction

This book originates in a series of playful conversations that we never took very seriously. Over about ten years, we have often discussed about the illusions of love, commenting on our own amatory ups and downs as well as those of our friends. At the beginning it was almost a joke. But the more we discussed, the more we agreed on some points that seemed interesting. This was rather surprising, since usually we disagree on almost everything. So we thought it might be a good idea to give a more theoretical form to our views. It quickly became clear that what we were doing was *epistemology of love*.

Epistemology is the branch of philosophy that studies the nature and limits of knowledge. The questions it addresses are those that arise when one reflects about the grounds of one's beliefs. We know that the Earth moves. But how do we know it? The belief that the Earth moves is justified; it is not like the belief that there is a yeti in the Himalayas. But why? What exactly are belief, justification, and knowledge? These are deep questions that have always been at the heart of philosophy.

Love is definitely one of the most intense human feelings, although perhaps not the most durable. Its power is so pervasive and widespread that it is almost impossible to imagine a loveless world. Many things people do, such as writing letters, buying rings or making long unnecessary phone calls, are the effects of love. The same goes for many things people say, as when they use the words 'passionate', ' mysterious' or ' beautiful person'. This is why it is natural to have *love beliefs*, that is, beliefs about our own loves and those of others.

The epistemology of love, as we understand it, includes any reflection on the grounds of love beliefs. Love beliefs are just like other beliefs. Some of them are grounded, some are not. Our work focuses on those of the second kind. Many love beliefs are like the belief that the yeti exists, in that they are built on clues that have roughly the same degree of reliability as a mark on snow resembling a big footprint. Lovers provide unequivocal examples of ungrounded beliefs, because love is an inexhaustible source of misperceptions, misconceptions and misunderstandings. The aim of this book is to identify and spell out some characteristic ways in which ungrounded love beliefs arise, are maintained and reinforced, and to illustrate some of the typical mistakes that constitute the main fallacies of love.

1

Basic notions

Amore, impossibile a definirsi.

GIACOMO CASANOVA[1]

1.1 What we talk about when we talk about love

The word 'love' can be used in many ways, but only some of them fall within the scope of our investigation. This book is about romantic love, the state that one experiences when one is 'in' love. Romantic love is an attitude that a person, the lover, has towards another person, the beloved, and that exhibits emotional and behavioural traits that distinguish it from friendship, family relations, or other kinds of attachment. Therefore, we will leave aside the use of 'love' in sentences such as 'I love my mother', 'I love my friends' or 'I love my students'. The ancient Greek had two words for 'love': *eros* was used to refer to a passionate desire for an individual, typically sexual desire; *philia*, instead, meant a kind of affectionate regard or feeling towards friends or family members. This book is about *eros*, it is not about *philia*.

In particular, we will be examining romantic love as distinct from the kind of attachment – call it 'conjugal love' – that typically sustains a stable relationship such as marriage. It is possible that two persons conjugally love each other without being in love, either because they are no longer in love, or because they have never been. Conversely, two persons can romantically love each other without ever forming a stable couple or standing in the relation of conjugal love. So, even though many people do not distinguish between conjugal love and romantic love, or talk about conjugal love as the one 'true' love, here we will reserve the word 'love' for romantic love.

We have said that love is an attitude that a person, the lover, has towards another person, the beloved. But what kind of attitude? The hypothesis that we will adopt is that love is a *dispositional state*: the lover has a characteristic set of dispositions that somehow involve the beloved. The term 'disposition' refers to a property that is defined in terms of what would happen in possible circumstances. For example, fragility is such a property. A glass is fragile in that it has a disposition to shatter when struck: if the glass were struck, it would shatter. The properties that characterize love are like fragility, as they have to do with how the lover would feel or behave in possible circumstances.

This means that it is not essential that the lover actually manifests some distinctive pattern of emotions or behaviour. Just as a glass can be fragile even though it is actually intact, if it has not been strucked, a person can love even though he or she does not actually feel or behave in any distinctive way.

At least three kinds of dispositions are usually associated with love. First, lovers typically manifest physical reactions caused by an interaction with the beloved. For example, a recurrent phenomenon they experience is an increase in heart rate and body temperature. The following verses provide a vivid description of similar symptoms:

He seems to me equal to the gods
that man who sits in front of you
and listens to your sweet voice
and smiles softly
that suddenly makes my heart throb
for when I glance at you even for a moment,
I can no longer speak,
my tongue is broken,
a subtle flame runs under my skin,
my eyes don't see,
a whirring noise fills my ears,
cold sweat holds me,
trembling seizes all my body,

I become paler than straw

And I feel as if I were about to die

SAPPHO, *Fragment* 31

Other physical reactions might be added to the list, such as the sensation that is sometimes described as 'butterflies in the stomach'. Pier Paolo Pasolini once wrote in a letter to a friend: 'I don't know what's happening to my stomach. Either it is gastritis or I fell in love again.' In any case, there is no need to provide a detailed description of the physical reactions that characterize love. For present purposes it would suffice to recognize that such reactions exist, that they may vary person to person, and that they can properly be explained at the neurophysiological level.[2]

Second, lovers are typically inclined to have intimate, repeated and prolonged sexual contact with the beloved. By 'repeated' we mean that the lover desires not just a single episode of sexual intercourse, but an indefinite number thereof. By 'prolonged' we mean that the lover tends to prolong each episode and, when possible, spend time with the beloved before and after each intercourse, sharing activities that are not directly sexual. Quite often, when we watch a film, we understand that two characters are in love with each other when we see a scene of passionate sex followed by a joking conversation in bed (with or without cigarettes), or a joyful breakfast together. The two characters tend to draw out their sexual interactions, and the time they spend together is motivated simply by the desire to be together.

Third, lovers are typically apt to act or think in strange or anomalous ways. When one is in love, one often manifests a tendency to do 'crazy' things, that is, things that one would never do if one were not in love. As William Shakespeare wrote:

If thou remember'st not the slightest folly
That ever love did make thee run into,
Thou has not loved.
            W. SHAKESPEARE, *As You Like It*, II, iv.

Obviously, what we perceive as crazy may vary from person to person. If Alex never drives a car and is afraid to do so, it would be crazy for Alex to drive 100 kilometres to meet someone on a date, while the same action may not be crazy for Kiko, who likes cars and has a brand new Lamborghini. But the fact remains that love induces each person to act or think in ways that are strange or anomalous for that person. Even though what counts as crazy for Alex may differ from what counts as crazy for Kiko, under the effect of love Alex is more likely to do things that are crazy for Alex, and Kiko is more likely to do things that are crazy for Kiko.

Moreover, there are recurrent ways of being crazy, which may easily affect Alex and Kiko independently of their individual differences. When one is in love, one is often willing to act in ways that go against one's self-interest, a willingness which diminishes when one is not in love. There are deeds that the lover decides to perform for the sake of the beloved (the sacrifice of Violetta for Alfredo in *La traviata*), but also actions of the beloved which harm the lover and which he or she would never accept in other circumstances. More importantly, when one is in love, one is often inclined to form irrational beliefs. Our book focuses precisely on such beliefs. The following chapters provide a detailed anatomy of the tendency to form ungrounded love beliefs.[3]

From now on we will assume that love is characterized by a set of dispositions that includes the three kinds of dispositions considered. This is not intended as a definition. We are not trying to provide necessary and sufficient conditions for love. It is at least conceivable that one can love without having some of the dispositions considered, or that one can have all the dispositions considered without loving. What we want to say is that those dispositions are typically associated with love. Perhaps we could add to the list the desire to be the only one for the beloved, which is the origin of the passion of jealousy, or the inclination to spend time with the beloved and share experiences that are part of the lover's life. But for present purposes it is not necessary to specify a complete list of dispositions. In what follows we will simply talk about the dispositions that characterize love – *love dispositions* – without referring to any specific disposition or set of dispositions.[4]

1.2 Some fundamental properties of love

Some properties commonly attributed to love can easily be described in terms of dispositions. First, love is traditionally classified as a *passion*, that is, as a state that one undergoes, rather than anything one actively does. Love is not subject to the will. If one loves a person, one cannot refrain from loving that person. Similarly, if one does not love a person, one cannot decide to love that person. This is consistent with the hypothesis that love is a dispositional state. One's dispositions towards a person are not something that one actively chooses, there is simply nothing one can do about them.[5]

Second, love is not really definable in terms of some characteristic *feel*. Although passions are generally understood to involve a phenomenological component, they cannot be reduced to such components. When one judges whether a person is in love, one's judgement is largely based on one's knowledge of the person's behaviour. This also holds for the case in which the person is oneself. When one retrospectively looks at one's past relationships, one often bases one's judgements on the observation of one's past actions, rather than on the reminiscence of one's past feelings. This is consistent with the hypothesis that love is a dispositional state. One's dispositions towards a person are manifested in one's behaviour, although they may be accompanied by a characteristic feel.

Third, love, like any passion, varies in intensity and strength. When one loves a person, one's love for that person comes into existence at some point, then increases, decreases and finally ceases to exist. So, if before and after this lapse of time the degree of one's love is zero, during the lapse it goes from zero to some higher degree. Moreover, people often make comparative judgements about the strength or intensity of different love relationships. For example, you may think that you love your present partner more than your former partner (or the other way round). People also compare love relationships with other kinds of relationships. According to common sense, loving a person is stronger, or more intense, than merely liking that person or having sex with that person. This is consistent with the hypothesis that love is a dispositional state, because dispositions are properties that allow for degrees.

Fourth, love is *non-symmetric*: although there are happy cases of requited love, it happens quite often that one loves without being loved, or that one loves without being loved with equal intensity. This is the tragedy of love. A tragedy, as commonly understood, is an inevitable suffering which strikes people against their will. Since love is a passion, people are doomed to suffer when their love is unrequited: there is no way to escape the pains, disappointments and broken hearts caused by unrequited love. This, again, is consistent with the hypothesis that love is a dispositional state, because dispositions are non-symmetric. One can have certain dispositions towards a person, even though that person does not have similar dispositions, or has similar dispositions but to a considerably lower degree.

What we have said so far about love may diverge to some extent from what past and present philosophers have said on this topic. Several definitions of love have been discussed in philosophy. According to one of them, to love is basically to care about the beloved. According to another, what is essential to love is the formation of some kind of union. According to a third definition, love is a matter of acknowledging and responding in a distinctive way to the value of the beloved. The characterization of love suggested here differs from such claims in at least two respects. One is that philosophical accounts of love tend to blur the distinction between *eros* and *philia*, whereas we want to maintain that distinction. As long as *philia* is left out of the picture, love can hardly be defined in terms of care about the beloved. The other is that philosophical accounts of love tend to rely more or less explicitly on some ideal of love, as they seem to define the good love, or love as it should be. Perhaps ideal love consists in forming a union, or perhaps there is good love only when the lover appropriately responds to the value of the beloved. But this book is about love, it is not about the good love. It deals with love as it actually is, leaving aside what it could or should be.[6]

1.3 Truth, justification and knowledge

The existence of love dispositions is a fact that we will take for granted. Some persons love other persons, and it is reasonable to presume that the dispositions they manifest have a causal history that can be elucidated by means of empirical data drawn from biology, psychology or sociology. Our work focuses on what people think about this fact. More precisely, we will draw attention to some ways in which the lover and the beloved may acquire ungrounded beliefs about themselves. As the word 'ungrounded' suggests, we adopt a normative perspective that implies a distinction between what is correct to think and what is not correct to think. This perspective can be framed by using some basic vocabulary from epistemology.

Normally, people express beliefs by uttering sentences. For example, the belief that snow is white can be expressed by uttering the sentence 'Snow is white'. When one utters a sentence, one says that things are a certain way. The sentence is *true* if things are actually that way, while it is *false* if things are not actually in that way. Schematically, if one says that *p* by uttering a sentence, then the sentence is true if and only if it is the case that p. Beliefs can be true or false just like the sentences that express them. The belief that p – just like the sentence 'p' – is true if and only if p.

To say that a belief is *justified*, on the other hand, is to say that there are reasons to think that the belief is true. A justified belief is acquired through a reliable method, that is, a method that generally leads to truth rather than to falsity. For example, visual perception is reliable. In normal circumstances, if you think that you are seeing a palm tree, it is because there really is a palm tree in front of you. By contrast, dreams are unreliable, as there is no similar correlation between the images of palm trees that occur in dreams and real palm trees.

Truth and justification are independent of each other. A belief can be justified without being true, because a reliable method is not necessarily infallible. Conversely, a belief can be true without being justified, because an unreliable method can accidentally lead to truth. Our investigation mainly concerns justification rather than truth. When we say that love beliefs may be ungrounded, we mean that they may be unjustified.

Moreover, we will talk about justification only as a property of beliefs, leaving aside other uses of the word 'justification'. Although it is reasonable to expect that some intelligible notion of justification can be applied to actions or emotions, we will not consider any such notion. More specifically, we will not address the question of whether one can have reasons to love a given person. We are concerned with the justification of love beliefs rather than with the justification of love itself.[7]

In most cases, when a subject has a belief that is both true and justified, it is legitimate to ascribe *knowledge* to the subject. Knowledge is hard to define, and we will not try to define it here. We are happy to leave the issue of the nature of knowledge to works on epistemology that do *not* deal with love. For present purposes it will suffice to bear in mind that most accounts of knowledge agree on at least two points. First, while belief can be true or false, knowledge entails truth. If one knows that *p*, then it is true that *p*. Second, while belief can be justified or unjustified, knowledge entails justification. If one knows that *p*, then one is justified in believing that *p*. In other words, truth and justification are necessary for knowledge. If it is false that *p*, or one is not justified in believing that *p*, then one does not know that *p*.

A last distinction that deserves attention is between *first-order beliefs*, such as Alex's belief that snow is white, and *second-order beliefs*, such as Kiko's belief that Alex believes that snow is white. Second-order beliefs, unlike first-order beliefs, are about other beliefs or other mental states. Thus, if Kiko believes that Alex believes that snow is white, Kiko's belief is a second-order belief about Alex's belief that snow is white. Similarly, if Alex believes that she believes that snow is white, Alex has a second-order belief about her own belief that snow is white. First-order and second-order beliefs are alike in one important respect: both kinds of beliefs can be true or false, justified or unjustified.

1.4 The fallacies of love

The fact that second-order beliefs can be unjustified is crucial for our investigation, because lovers can be wrong about their own mental states. Love is not epistemically transparent. It is not necessarily the case that if one is in love, then one knows that one is in love. It may happen that one is in love but that one has no adequate evidence for thinking that one is in love, because one has not yet shown any noticeable emotional or behavioural pattern. Similarly, it is not necessarily the case that if one is not in love, then one knows that one is not in love. It may happen that one misinterprets one's actions or emotions as a sign of love when they are really a sign of something else, such as admiration or strong sexual interest.

Of course, many people are inclined to think otherwise. First-person authority is often invoked to justify claims about love, as in sentences such as 'Only I can know how much I love you', 'I love you and I know what I'm saying' or 'If you really loved me, you would know'. In general, it is common to think that nobody can know one's own emotional state better than oneself. But this way of thinking is misguided, or so we will propose. Although in many cases one knows much about one's emotional state, it is not true that one is always in a position to know one's emotional state better than any other person. This is indeed just what we would expect on the hypothesis that love is a dispositional state: one is not always able to know one's dispositions better than any other person. As noted in Section 1.2, it happens quite often that the evidence about oneself that one gets from a third-person point of view overrides the first-person assessment of what one feels.[8]

We can now state the idea that will be developed in the next chapters: *love talk is deceptive*. When one talks about matters of love in which one is involved, one often tends to make assertions that may easily foster unjustified beliefs. Of course, this is due at least in part to the fact that people may lie about their feelings. But the important point – the point we want to emphasize – is that people often make misleading assertions in spite of being sincere. This is to say that they are subject to some form of self-deception.

The kind of situation that we have in mind may be described as follows. There is a love relationship between two persons. One of them sincerely utters a sentence '*p*', which expresses a love belief, and thinks that there are reasons for believing that *p*. This may easily induce the other person to believe that *p*. But in reality there is no reason to believe that *p*. As it will turn out clearly, situations of this kind show that love talk may be deceptive. The fact that one of the two persons sincerely says that p does not justify the other person to believe that p. In the following chapters we shall see how the failure to recognize the gap between what people say and what there is reason to believe is the main source of the fallacies of love, that is, of the unjustified beliefs that typically affect lovers.[9]

The reason why it is important to recognize unjustified love beliefs is obvious. Justification is a guide to truth: if a belief is justified, then it is probable that it is true. Since actions are based on beliefs, it is generally better to have true beliefs than false beliefs. For example, if Alex has no reasons for believing that he will get a pay raise, then it is better for him not to believe that he will. If Alex did believe it, he could buy a new car but then realize that he does not have the money to pay for it. The same goes for love beliefs. Suppose that Alex has a crush on Kiko, who spends a lot of time with him but is not attracted to him at all. If Alex has no reasons for believing that Kiko will turn her attentions to him and leave her long-standing boyfriend Jules, as he desires, then it is better for him not to believe it. If he did believe it, he might invest too much of his time and energy in a project without a future.

Some readers might be tempted to object that any consideration about the importance of justification is totally out of place in the realm of love, because love is a mystery. Justification requires understanding, while love cannot be understood. When one loves, one must simply let oneself go and abandon one's critical faculties. Loving is like drinking, gambling or free climbing. What makes it exciting is just the absence of rationality. Unjustified beliefs, therefore, are just part of the magic of love: if they make us feel good, there is no reason to abandon them. So, for example, it might be contended that it is irrelevant that Alex has no justification for believing that Kiko will break up with Jules. All that matters is how Alex feels. And if the belief that Kiko will break up with Jules makes him feel good, then it is good for him to believe it.

Although this objection expresses a common way of thinking, it is not convincing. First, it is far from obvious that feeling good without knowing is better than knowing without feeling good. After all, if Kiko has no intention to break up with Jules, wouldn't it be better for Alex to know it? Second, and more importantly, unjustified love beliefs may easily cause pain, sadness and frustration. If Kiko has no intention of breaking up with Jules, sooner or later Alex will realize it, and he will fall into a state of sorrow that might be stronger than the joy that he experiences now.

We are not saying that it is wrong to let go. We are not against drinking, gambling or free climbing. There is nothing intrinsically bad about doing risky things, as long as one has a sufficiently clear idea of one's margin for failure. What we want to say about the case of Alex is not that he should stop seeing

Kiko, or that he should not desire her to leave Jules. The point is simply that he should not indulge in fantasies about Kiko that rely on the unjustified belief that she will break up with Jules. Doing so may be bad for him.

Nor are we saying that having unjustified love beliefs is always wrong, or that such beliefs should always be avoided. Presumably, there are cases in which unjustified love beliefs produce no considerable losses and determine courses of actions that are beneficial in the long run. However, generally speaking, unjustified love beliefs have negative consequences.

1.5 Sex, gender and stereotypes

The examples that we will use in the following chapters to illustrate the fallacies of love concern real persons, literary characters and our imaginary individuals Alex, Kiko and Jules. Some of these examples are modelled on stereotypes, as they reproduce paradigmatic or standardized situations that are traditionally associated with love. More generally, we will deliberately draw on the clichés of love that we find in our cultural heritage. Since stereotypes do not do justice to the variety and complexity of actual love relationships, and may give rise to misunderstandings and misinterpretations, it is useful to provide some explanations.

One thing that must be clarified about our examples is that they are not intended to suggest that the fallacies of love are gender sensitive. Although we use 'he' in some cases and 'she' in other cases, the pronouns could be switched without any loss. Of course it is possible that there are gender differences with respect to the propensity to make certain mistakes. Or at least, we have no reason to rule out that possibility. But we do not intend to speculate about such correlations. Moreover, and more importantly, our main goal is to identify and describe some characteristic mistakes, so we are interested in the mistakes themselves, rather than in who commits them.

Another thing that must be clarified is that the gender polarity that emerges from our examples does not imply that we take heterosexuality for granted. Most of these examples involve roles that are traditionally attributed to men and women, but that are not necessarily instantiated by males and females. As far as we are concerned, Alex, Kiko and Jules can equally be male or female, and this is why we use unisex dummy names. It is not even essential for us to assume gender polarity as it is traditionally understood. The very idea that a love relationship implies two genders may itself be regarded as a stereotype. So we can easily imagine similar examples that involve two males or two females. The fallacies of love as we will describe them are insensitive to the distinction between heterosexuality and homosexuality.

Our examples are sometimes modelled on stereotypes for at least three reasons. First, the good thing about stereotypes is that everybody is familiar with them, so they make it easy to sketch common types of situations without providing many details or explanations. Second, stereotypes provide a wide collection of cases that deserve careful attention, so an epistemological analysis of love must deal with them. As a matter of fact, it is reasonable to expect that if any such analysis works, then it must work when applied to the stereotypical cases we present. Third, the use of stereotypes may have interesting implications concerning the perception of the stereotypes themselves. Understanding the cognitive mistakes that characterize a stereotypical situation has a demystifying effect. It helps us to perceive more clearly what is wrong in that situation.[10]

1.6 Some final remarks

So far, we have provided some preliminary clarifications in order to explain what this book is about. What remains to be said is what this book is *not* about. First, there will be no room for panegyrics of love. We will not praise love for its depth, for its beauty or for its ethical or existential significance. That has already been done abundantly by poets, writers and singers. Moreover, as explained in Section 1.2, we will not offer any ideal of love. For us, the existence of love dispositions is a fact that can be taken for granted in order to elucidate some cognitive mistakes. This is not to suggest that love is a bad thing, or that people should not love. Love has many qualities, the fact is simply that we will not talk about them.

Second, we have no definite answer to the question whether our book has appreciable practical consequences. Our aim is primarily theoretical. This is a book for those who want to know more about the cognitive mistakes that people make when they are in love. Even assuming that such mistakes are to be avoided, the utility of our work is very limited. In general, knowing a certain cognitive mistake does not prevent one from making that mistake. If you are in love and you have unjustified beliefs, it is very unlikely that a book will make you abandon those beliefs. Usually, when people stop committing a certain mistake, it is because they have experienced the negative consequences of that mistake, not because they have devoted some time to epistemological reflections.

Third, we will not take into account the evolution of love as a social and anthropological phenomenon, or the cultural and geographical diversity of love relationships. The actions and thoughts related to love may vary considerably across time and cultures. The way lovers behaved in ancient Rome may have been different from the way lovers behave in contemporary Rome, and the way lovers behave today in China may differ from the way lovers behave today in New Zealand. However, the existence of such differences by itself does not entail that there is significant variation at the epistemological level. Although we are open to the possibility that some accurate inquiry will show that in different historical periods, or in different countries, lovers make different cognitive mistakes, it seems plausible that human beings are all alike as far as self-deception and other forms or irrationality are concerned. Or at least, it is reasonable to conjecture that there is a core of cognitive propensities that are universal, those that we find illustrated in the literature of many historical periods and cultures.[11]

2

The invention of reasons

The mind seeks to bring the facts, as modified by the new discovery, into order; that is, to form a general conception embracing them, … so that the phenomenon, under that assumption, would not be surprising, but quite likely, or even would be a necessary result.

C. S. PEIRCE, *A SYLLABUS OF CERTAIN TOPICS OF LOGIC*

2.1 Rationalization

Everybody wants to be rational. Normally, when one performs an action or experiences an emotion, one tends to think that one's action or emotion is explained by some reasonable motivation. An explanation of this kind may satisfy one's need for self-understanding and may be used to justify one's behaviour or feelings before other people. However, this natural tendency to look for explanations may generate distortions and misperceptions. Quite often, the real motivations of one's actions or emotions are not exactly those one attributes to oneself.

In psychology, the term *rationalization* is used to indicate the mental process by which a subject attempts to provide a coherent explanation of an action or emotion of which he or she does not recognize – or does not want to recognize – the real causes. This term comes from the vocabulary of psychoanalysis, where it was introduced to denote a mechanism of 'defence' by which a subject tries to justify an action or emotion whose real causes are subconscious. However, we will talk about rationalization in the first, more generic sense as sketched above, without relying on any psychoanalytic theory or assumption.[1] Aesop's fable *The Fox and the Grapes* provides a clear example of rationalization:

> Driven by hunger, a fox tried to get its paws on some grapes hanging high on the vine but was unable to do so, although he tried with all his strength. As he went away, the fox remarked 'Oh you aren't even ripe yet! I don't need any sour grapes'.[2]

The fox suffers a reversal, because he is unable to reach the grapes. But since he does not want to admit his defeat, he tries to provide an alternative explanation of his behaviour, saying that he is no longer attempting to eat the grapes because they are sour. This explanation makes him feel better.

Note that Aesop's fable may be interpreted in two ways. Either the fox says that the grapes are sour because he really has come to believe that they are sour, or he says that the grapes are sour without believing it, just to hide or forget his failure. Here, we will adopt the first interpretation. This is not to suggest that the first interpretation is more plausible than the second from an exegetical or psychological point of view. The reason is simply that the second interpretation is irrelevant for our purposes. As we said in Section 1.4, we are not interested in lies. The cases of rationalization that we will discuss are cases in which people really believe what they say.

The psychological mechanism of rationalization plays a crucial role in the formation of unjustified love beliefs. In most cases, unjustified love beliefs are fostered by the need to explain why the lover or the beloved performs certain actions or experiences certain emotions. In this chapter, we shall present some common fallacies that show the effects of rationalization on love beliefs.

2.2 The you–you fallacy

The first fallacy that we shall consider is the *you–you fallacy*. One commits this fallacy when one tries to explain one's love for a person by appealing to some alleged intrinsic value of that person, that is, some value that is not reducible to actual qualities of that person. This way one fails to recognize that one's love for that person would be considerably weaker, or would not exist at all, if that person had different properties. In other words, one believes that one's love for a person does not depend on the fact that that person has certain properties, even though one has no reason to believe this. The following dialogue illustrates this kind of mistake:

Kiko: Don't you see that I want to be with you? I love *you*, everything else doesn't matter. I don't care that you are a photographer, that you are stylish and good-looking, or that you live in this beautiful penthouse. I would love you anyway.

Alex: Really?

Kiko: Believe me. I know what I'm saying. I love you because it's you, not because of what you do or what you have.

Alex: But why me? What do you find in me?

Kiko: There is something that you have and that the others don't have.

Alex: I understand.

In fact, Alex has not understood anything. If he has an interesting job, dresses well, is not ugly, and his apartment is attractive, it is quite unlikely that all this does not matter. We are not saying that Kiko is lying. Presumably, she really thinks that she loves him just because he is who he is. But this does not mean that what she says is true. The questions on which Alex should reflect are the following: If instead of being a photographer he was a street trader selling pigeon feed, would she have fallen in love with him? If he wore socks with sandals, or were 30 kilos fatter, would she be attracted to him? And, if he lived in a shabby basement, or his house were crowded with malodorous pets, would it be the same for her? If the answer to some of these questions is negative, then what he does and what he has do matter. Moreover, even assuming that the properties just mentioned do not mean anything to her, which is quite unlikely, this does not rule out that there are other properties of him that do matter for her.

The you–you fallacy fosters unjustified beliefs that can have disastrous effects. If one comes to believe that the love that one receives from a person does not depend on one's actual properties, one will be inclined to take that love for granted, as if it could not be affected by any change in those properties. But this line of action can produce undesired alterations in the other person's love dispositions. Imagine that Alex and Kiko, after living together for some time, have serious problems because he spends every night at home watching sports or playing videogames with his friends. This is a possible sequel of our story:

Kiko: I can't stand you anymore, we are finished!

Alex: What's wrong? Can you tell me what is not working?

Kiko: Something has changed, you …

Alex: I … what?

Kiko: You … are not the man I fell in love with.

Alex: What do you mean?

Kiko: You … are no longer you.

Alex: I don't get it.

This dialogue shows the kind of misunderstanding that is typically caused by the you–you fallacy. First, let us consider what Alex may have in mind. Since Alex believes that Kiko loved him as an individual, independently of his properties, he cannot understand why her attitude has changed now. The feeling that Kiko manifested in the past should not change as a consequence of the fact that Alex is now watching sports and playing videogames with his friends, for Alex is still Alex. If she loved me because it was me – he must think – why doesn't she keep loving me? Besides – he might ask – what does it mean that I am not myself?

Now let us consider what Kiko may have in mind. Since Kiko believed that she loved Alex as an individual, independently of his properties, it is hard for her to explain why she is vacillating now. If Alex is the same individual as before, she should continue to love him. This is why Kiko comes up with the obvious falsity that Alex is not Alex. Of course Alex is Alex, the same man she fell in love with. The fact is simply that some of his properties have changed, or perhaps that his real properties are not exactly those she used to think he had.

The only way to avoid this kind of misunderstanding is to recognize that the properties of the beloved do matter for the lover. William Butler Yeats was certainly aware of this fact when he wrote the following verses:

> I heard an old religious man
> But yesternight declare
> That he had found a text to prove
> That only God, my dear,
> Could love you for yourself alone
> And not your yellow hair.

W. B. YEATS, *For Anne Gregory*

When one loves a person, there is a set of properties of that person that are causally related to one's dispositions and therefore explain one's love. The problem is that most of the time one is unable to identify with clarity the properties that determine one's love for a person, and consequently one is unable to understand how a change in such properties may affect one's attitude towards that person.

2.3 The virtue fallacy

The second fallacy that we shall consider, the *virtue fallacy*, is related to the same lack of clarity about the properties of the beloved that emerges in the first fallacy. In this case, however, one tries to explain one's love for a person by appealing to valuable properties of that person. The mistake is due to the fact that one has no reasons for thinking that the properties mentioned in the explanation are really the properties that are causally relevant for one's love. The following dialogue provides an example:

Alex: Do you know what I like about you? You are a sensitive and thoughtful person, you understand people. Especially with kids, you always know what to do.

Kiko: Yes, I adore kids.

Alex: But you also are a strong and independent spirit. You always know what you want.

Kiko: Yes, that is the sort of person I am.

Alex: I love you because you are like this. I could never be with a different kind of person.

Kiko: So good to hear that you love me for who I am.

This time, Kiko is the one who has not understood anything. Alex is trying to explain his love for her by appealing to some properties that he ascribes to her: sensitivity, thoughtfulness and strength of character. He certainly believes what he says, and maybe he is right: we are not questioning Kiko's sensitivity, thoughtfulness or strength of character. However, it is very likely that Alex's love for Kiko is not explainable simply in terms of those properties. On the one hand, many persons are equally sensitive, thoughtful and have a strong character, even though he is not equally attracted to them. Perhaps he would not love a person who had those properties but were much uglier than her, or much more pretentious. On the other hand, many persons are significantly less sensitive, thoughtful and have weak characters, even though he may be attracted to them. Perhaps he would love a person who lacked those properties but were much prettier than her, or much less pretentious. Therefore, Alex's love for Kiko depends on a set of properties that is not exactly that mentioned in his explanation. This set might include her voice, her smile or her way of moving. Who knows? We certainly do not. But neither does Alex.

The negative effects of the virtue fallacy are similar to those of the you–you fallacy. If one comes to believe that the love that one receives from a person depends on certain properties that one actually has, one will be inclined to think that, as long as one maintains those properties, that love cannot decrease or disappear. But this way of thinking often produces undesired consequences, because one may easily be wrong about the properties that explain the other person's love dispositions.

The you–you fallacy and the virtue fallacy are two typical mistakes that lovers tend to make when they think about their love. In both cases, the source of the mistake is the psychological mechanism of rationalization, because lovers try to provide satisfactory explanations in spite of the fact that they are largely unaware of the real causes of their dispositions. The difference between the two fallacies lies in the kind of explanation provided: in the first case the explanation does not take into account the causally relevant properties of the beloved because it appeals to the individuality of the beloved, while in the second case it does not take into account such properties because it appeals to other properties of the beloved that the lover regards as valuable.

The two kinds of explanations considered have an obvious justificatory function. An explanation of an action or emotion counts as a justification when the causes it indicates provide reasons for the action or emotion. Generally, the lover is apt to think that there are reasons for loving the beloved, that is, that the beloved really deserves to be loved. Very often, this way of thinking induces the lover to believe that the beloved is special, where 'special' is to be understood in some objective and non-trivial sense. Here, 'objective' means that what is taken to be special about the beloved can at least in principle be recognized by persons other than the lover, and 'non-trivial' means that what is special about the beloved is not merely that the beloved instantiates a unique set of properties or is related to the lover in a unique way. Note that if 'special' were not understood in some objective and non-trivial sense, the claim that the beloved is special would be an insignificant truth and could play no justificatory role. The you–you fallacy and the virtue fallacy are nothing but common ways in which lovers form the belief that their beloved is special.

Certainly, it is exciting, pleasant and invigorating for the lover to believe that the beloved is special. When one has a belief of this kind, one can swallow pills that one would not be willing to swallow otherwise. This dialogue will sound familiar to some readers:

Alex: I saw her last night. We went to the theater, then we went for a long walk. I had a very good time.

Jules: A *walk*? Didn't you go home with her? Nothing happened?

Alex: Not yet. But it will, sooner or later.

Jules: Can't you hurry things up?

Alex: Maybe she is not ready …

Jules: Ready? What are you waiting for?

Alex: She is different.

Jules: What's different about her?

Alex: She … is special.

The belief that the beloved is special is often combined with another belief that is also exciting, pleasant and invigorating for the lover, the belief that there is something special in the relation itself that ties the lover to the beloved. When lovers tell the story of their love, they tend to make it appear unique or exceptional, pretty much in the same way in which the idealized love stories that they find in films and novels are unique or exceptional. This adds an extra value to their choice, and makes them feel better.

Unfortunately, when lovers believe that their beloved is special, or that their love story is special, they typically believe it without justification. Even if some lovers may be accidentally right – some people are really loveable, and some love stories are really out of the ordinary – it is very unlikely that all lovers be right. The property of being special, if it makes sense to talk about such a property, belongs to some people only if it does not belong to most people. In other words, it is like the property of being very tall or the property of having an IQ well above average. Remember that here 'special' is understood in some objective and non-trivial sense. Since most people have been loved by some people, most people have been regarded as special by some people. Therefore, if all lovers were right, then most people would be special.

To sum up, the you–you fallacy and the virtue fallacy are two common mistakes that lovers tend to make when they rationalize their actions or emotions. To recognize these fallacies is to understand that it is naively optimistic to think that the beloved is special. Consequently, it is naively optimistic for the beloved to think that he or she is special. Obviously, the belief that the beloved is special may be comfortable for the lover, as noted above, and also for the beloved. But comfort has a price.

A comfortable belief may have unpleasant consequences that make it preferable to live without it.[3]

2.4 Purported sour grapes

So far, we have considered two fallacies that lovers tend to commit when they try to make sense of their love. Now we shall present three other fallacies that involve rationalization. In each of the three cases, the lover believes that things are a certain way because he or she wrongly assumes that the hypothesis that things are that way provides an explanation of some facts. As we shall see in the rest of this chapter and in the next, the fallacious ways in which lovers acquire unjustified beliefs often resemble ways of acquiring beliefs that are not fallacious. The power of some fallacies is due precisely to the fact that lovers tend to mistake fallacious ways of acquiring beliefs for reliable methods that bear some resemblance to them.

In Section 2.1, we used the fable of the fox and the grapes to introduce the notion of rationalization. This fable is interesting not only because it helps to explain in general terms what rationalization is, but also because it illustrates a specific form of rationalization that is quite widespread among dissatisfied lovers. Typically, when one's love is unrequited, one may easily indulge in unjustified beliefs about the beloved that play some consolatory role, that is, beliefs that ascribe to the beloved some negative property that makes it easier for the lover to accept the lack of reciprocity. Dissatisfied lovers often behave like the fox, as they say things such as 'She does not deserve me', 'It was not going to work anyway' or 'He was not so smart after all'.

The mental process involved in this mistake, the *fox fallacy*, may be described as follows. Initially, one has a desire. Then it becomes clear that the desire will not be satisfied. As a consequence of this, one starts believing without justification that the object of the desire has some property that makes it undesirable. Think about the fox. Initially, the fox desires the grapes. But as soon as he realizes that he is unable to reach them, he starts believing that they are sour. Obviously, he has no justification for believing that they are sour. The fact is simply that believing that they are sour makes him feel better, because sour grapes are not desirable.

Here, 'desirable' stands for 'pleasant', 'attractive' or 'appealing', it does not stand for 'good', 'valuable' or 'beneficial'. Although both kinds of properties can make something desirable, only the first matters for the fox. If 'desirable' were understood in the second sense, the undesirability of the grapes would be consistent with his initial desire. The fox could keep desiring the grapes in the first sense even if he believed that they are not desirable in the second sense. After all, many smokers keep desiring their cigarette, in spite of their belief that smoking is not good for them.

It is important to note that it is not irrational for the fox to change his initial desire, given his belief that the grapes are sour. The modification of the fox's initial desire is not a direct consequence of the fact that he cannot grasp the grapes. Rather, it is a direct consequence of the belief that the grapes are sour, which causally depends on that fact. To put it another way, the mental process that leads the fox to change his initial desire may be divided into two steps: first he acquires the belief that the grapes are sour, then he stops desiring the grapes on the basis of this belief. The fox is irrational when he takes the first step, not in the second step.[4]

The fox fallacy is a mistake that occurs whenever the lover, moved by some frustrated desire, acquires consolatory unjustified beliefs that ascribe negative properties to the beloved, that is, beliefs that are analogous to the fox's belief that the grapes are sour. It is important to note that this case differs from at least two cases that resemble it in some respects. First, it differs from the case in which the lover, moved by a frustrated desire, is inclined to acquire consolatory beliefs that have nothing to do with the beloved. For example, a dissatisfied lover may find consolation in the unjustified belief that he or she will find a better person to love, or that his or her career prospects will improve. Second, it differs from the case in which the lover, moved by a frustrated desire, is inclined to strengthen consolatory pre-existing beliefs that are justified. For example, it may be consolatory for a dissatisfied lover to remember or emphasize some noticeable flaws of the beloved, but in so doing the lover makes no cognitive mistake.

2.5 Lost love's labours

Yo no la quería cuando la encontré,
hasta que una noche me dijo, resuelta:
Ya estoy muy cansada de todo ... y se fue.
¡Qué cosas, hermano, que tiene la vida!
Desde ese momento la empecé a querer.[5]

L. C. AMADORI, *Quién hubiera dicho*

A rather different case, which contrasts with the fox fallacy, is that in which the lover starts valuing the beloved only after the beloved is gone. The tango song quoted above tells the story of a man who is tormented by the memory of a woman who loved him for two years. He did not love her when she was with him, but started loving her after she left him, when it was too late. Since the night in which she walked away, he tries in vain to forget her. This story differs significantly from the story of the fox. The fox initially desires the grapes, but when he realizes that he cannot reach them, he starts thinking that they are not desirable. The man in the tango song, on the other hand, initially does not desire the woman, but when he realizes that she is gone, he starts thinking that she is desirable. Situations of this kind are rather common. Another clear example is provided by the film *Manhattan*, by Woody Allen. Isaac becomes deeply attracted to his young girlfriend Tracy just after he has broken off his relationship with her, when she decides to leave for London.

The mistake that one commits in such a case, the *lost love fallacy*, may be described as follows. Initially, one does not desire a given person. Then that person becomes unavailable, and as a consequence of this, one starts believing that that person is desirable. Independently of whether one really desires that person or merely believes that that person is desirable, in some respects this case is opposite to the case of the fox fallacy. Instead of coming to believe that something is not desirable because it is impossible, in this case one believes that something is desirable just because it is impossible. What happens here is perhaps an extreme manifestation of a well-known psychological phenomenon, the tendency to value things that are hard to obtain just because they are hard to obtain.

To see why a belief formed in this way may be unjustified, it is only necessary to remember that, when one starts desiring the lost person, that person may be exactly the same person as before. Normally, when one thinks that a person is desirable, one thinks that this is due to some physical or mental qualities of the person, such as beauty, goodness and so on. But if the lost person is exactly the same as before, any physical or mental quality that can now make that person desirable is a quality that that person already had before (there is, of course, the possibility that one unexpectedly notices some property of that person, such as being determined, just as a consequence of the breakup; but we are not considering this possibility). Therefore, if the lost person were really desirable in virtue of that property, one would have desired that person before.

One final remark. The case of the lost love fallacy differs from the case in which the lover comes to appreciate the depth or intensity of his or her love only after the beloved is gone. This is what happens, for example, in Marcel Proust's novel *In Search of Lost Time*. Initially, Marcel thinks that he no longer loves Albertine. But after Albertine's departure, he is overcome by a sense of grief and loss. He understands how much he loved her and still loves her. Clearly, Marcel is not like the man in the tango song, because he desires Albertine from the very beginning. What characterizes the lost love fallacy is that initially the lover does not desire the beloved.

2.6 Inference to the worst explanation

When Robinson Crusoe sees for the first time a man's footprint on the beach of his island, he is overwhelmed by a sense of fear and trepidation. He starts wondering about the possible causes of the footprint, and the first thought that crosses his mind is that it is the footprint of the devil. Subsequently, more careful reflections induce him to abandon that idea, and he comes to the conclusion that there has to be a savage who reached the island in canoe.

The reasoning that leads Robinson Crusoe to endorse the hypothesis of the savage is an inference to the best explanation. He observes a fact that calls for an explanation, the footprint, and he compares different hypotheses to see which of them provides the best explanation of that fact. Since he eventually recognizes that the hypothesis of the savage is the most plausible – it is unlikely that the devil left the footprint just to terrify him – this gives him a reason to believe that the hypothesis of the savage is true.

More sophisticated examples of inference to the best explanation can be found in the empirical sciences. Think about the theory of evolution. The fossil record – the remains or imprints of organisms from earlier geological periods preserved in sedimentary rock – is a fact in need of explanation. The fossils belong to different species, they are located in different regions and in different strata, and so on. A plausible explanation of this fact is provided by the hypothesis that animal species have evolved through natural selection. Obviously, this is not the only possible hypothesis. Fossils could have been created by God, or they could have been brought to earth by aliens. But these alternative hypotheses are definitely less likely. For all we know, the theory of evolution provides the best explanation of the fossil record, and this is why it is reasonable to believe in it.

The method of reasoning just illustrated yields justified beliefs when it is applied correctly, that is, when the hypothesis selected is really the best among those available in the epistemic context in which it is adopted. However, it may yield unjustified beliefs when it is not applied correctly. The last fallacy that we shall consider, the *inference to the worst explanation*, is the mistake that one commits when one tries to explain some facts by means of a hypothesis that is not really the best among those available in one's epistemic context. If the hypothesis endorsed is compared with the most plausible hypothesis available in one's epistemic context, it is definitely the worse of the two. This is why we use the word 'worst' in the name the fallacy, even if strictly speaking the hypothesis endorsed need not be absolutely the worst. Lovers often commit this mistake, as they behave like Robinson Crusoe when he agitatedly and unreflectively thinks that the footprint is a work of the devil.

The reason why lovers may lack insight into the explanatory options that are open to them is that their powers of discernment are limited by emotional factors. The situation that characterizes most cases of inference to the worst explanation may be described as follows. One has a desire that is not satisfied, and in order to explain the fact that the desire is not satisfied, one endorses a hypothesis that alleviates one's dissatisfaction, even though it does not provide the best explanation of the fact that the desire is not satisfied. In this respect, the case is not exactly like that of Robinson Crusoe, because thinking about the devil is definitely not pleasant.

Here are two examples of inference to the worst explanation. In both cases, the explanation provided is patently not the best, but is rather one that makes the lover feel better. First:

> Kiko and Jules have been dating for a year. Kiko is in love with Jules and wants him to commit himself to her. But when Kiko asks him to make his position clear, Jules steps back and says that he is not sure that he wants a serious relationship. Then Kiko thinks: 'He is immature.'

In this case, the fact to be explained is that Jules does not want to commit himself, and the explanatory hypothesis that Kiko favours is that Jules is immature. Of course, this hypothesis is not entirely implausible: if Jules were immature, then he would not commit himself to her. But the point is that there is another hypothesis that is clearly more plausible, namely, that Jules does not love her enough. Kiko does not, we may suppose, have independent reasons for thinking that the former hypothesis is more likely than the latter. Her real motivation is that the former hypothesis affects her self-esteem less than the latter.

The second example is the following:

Alex and Kiko have just met at a party and exchanged phone numbers. Alex is strongly attracted to Kiko and wants to ask her out. He calls her for the first time, but nobody answers. He waits and then tries again one, two, three times, but again nobody answers. He keeps calling her the day after and two days after, without any result. Then he thinks: 'Perhaps she has lost her phone.'

In this case, the fact to be explained is that Kiko does not return Alex's calls, and the explanatory hypothesis that occurs to Alex is that Kiko lost her phone. As in the previous case, this hypothesis is not entirely implausible: if Kiko had lost her phone, then she would not answer. But the point is that there is another hypothesis that is clearly more plausible, namely, that Kiko does not want to answer. Presumably, Alex does not have independent reasons for thinking that the former hypothesis is more likely than the latter. His real motivation is that the former hypothesis affects his self-esteem less than the latter.

3

The power of desire over belief

Forse era ver, ma non però credibile
a chi del senso suo fosse signore;
ma parve facilmente a lui possibile,
ch'era perduto in via più grave errore.
Quel che l'uom vede, Amor gli fa invisibile
e l'invisibil fa vedere Amore.
Questo creduto fu; che 'l miser suole
dar facile credenza a quel che vuole.

L. ARIOSTO, ORLANDO FURIOSO[1]

3.1 The glasses of love

As Chapter 2 suggests, love can easily distort our perception of reality. Lovers see the world through the glasses of love, which are quite unlike regular glasses. While regular glasses improve our sight by assisting or correcting our eyes, the glasses of love often dim our sight. They can change the appearance of the things we see, prevent us from seeing things that are in front of us, or make us see things that are not in front of us. This chapter aims to describe some forms of distortion that are widespread among lovers.

We will mainly focus on the misperceptions of reality caused by desire, which is the most powerful driving force in the lives of lovers. As our discussion of rationalization shows, lovers tend to believe things that make them feel better. In Section 2.4 we saw that when one's love is unrequited, one may easily indulge in unjustified beliefs about the beloved that play some consolatory role. Similarly, in Section 2.6 we saw that one may be apt to endorse an explanatory hypothesis that is less plausible than another only because it affects one's self-esteem less than the other. The common factor that plays a key role in such cases is the psychological mechanism of *wishful thinking*, which may be defined as the tendency to believe what one desires.

Wishful thinking is an inexhaustible source of unjustified love beliefs. Lovers naturally tend to think that things are a certain way only because they desire that things be that way, that is, without having any justification for believing it. This is not to say that their beliefs must be false. As we saw in Section 1.3, it is possible to believe that p without having a justification for believing that p, and nonetheless it is the case that p. The same goes for the other fallacies of love.

The next two sections illustrate two major effects of wishful thinking, that is, two major ways in which wishful thinking may affect love beliefs. Then, we shall consider a phenomenon that is analogous to wishful thinking but concerns perception rather than belief. Finally, we shall consider a cognitive mistake that involves a misperception of reality but which differs significantly from wishful thinking.

3.2 Belief without evidence

The first effect of wishful thinking is that one may believe that p, because one desires that p, even though one does not have enough evidence for believing that p. Here is an example:

Alex and Kiko work together, and Alex's friendship with Kiko has grown into love. Kiko behaves in a tender and loving way towards Alex, but does the same with other workmates too. In spite of the fact that Kiko shows no intention to go any further, and that her attentions are divided equally among everyone else in the office, Alex is flattered by her behaviour and thinks that she is attracted to him.

Alex is not justified in believing that Kiko is attracted to him, for her behaviour towards him provides no evidence that this is the case. The fact is that Alex believes in her attraction just because he would like it to be the case that she is attracted to him.

Note that the situation just described resembles to some extent a situation in which the belief is justified because the evidence is good enough. If Kiko were *particularly* tender and loving towards Alex, that is, if her attentions to him were significantly different from her attention to other workmates, it would be reasonable for him to think that she is attracted to him. This is why it is easy to fall into the trap of wishful thinking. Typically, in such a case one tends to overestimate the evidence for believing that things are a certain way simply because one desires things to be that way.

Sometimes the effects of wishful thinking are astonishing. The power of desire over belief is so strong that a person can end up believing things for which there is not a shred of evidence. In the series *The Big Bang Theory* there is a scene in which a boy, after being rejected several times by a girl who shows no interest in him, says that she behaves in this way precisely because she is attracted to him. Such gross misperceptions of reality are not rare. Dissatisfied lovers often say things such as 'She is dissimulating', 'She is shy and reserved' or 'He loves me but he is afraid of commitment'.

A rather familiar case of wishful thinking is that in which the lover is involved in a conversation with friends about a kind of action that he or she takes to be morally bad, and says that the beloved would never do that. Generally, in this case the lover does not have enough evidence for believing that the beloved would never do the action in question. The fact is that the lover wants to believe that this is the case. Of course, the lover may try to support his or her belief by appealing to some special qualities of the beloved. For example, married persons who had a few one-night stands and consider the possibility that their partner does the same may think: 'She would never have sex with someone she doesn't love.' But the attribution of special qualities to the beloved is itself in need of justification. Maybe she *would* have sex with someone she does not love.

Another common case of wishful thinking is that in which the lover says things such as 'I've never felt so good', 'Now I know what love is' or 'This time it's true love', for it often happens that there is no good evidence for believing such things. The lover, moved by desire, is inclined to believe that his or her present feeling is stronger than his or her past feelings, or that the beloved, all things considered, is better than other persons he or she loved in the past. Probably, this kind of unjustified belief also depends on a psychological phenomenon that differs from wishful thinking, the tendency to privilege present experiences above past experiences due to the immediateness of present experiences and to the limits of memory. For example, when people say, 'The summer here has never been so hot,' they are affected by this tendency. Nonetheless, wishful thinking always contributes to some extent towards shaping the image that lovers have of their own love.

At least some misunderstandings that occur in sentimental relationships are due to unjustified beliefs based on wishful thinking. The cases of unrequited love are typically cases in which the lover tends to interpret the actions of the beloved as manifestations of love. A friend of one of us had a recurring experience. He had several affairs, liaisons and flirtations with women he was not in love with. Each time, he said to the woman of the moment that he was not in love with her and carefully avoided any action that could suggest the contrary. But each time she interpreted any gesture of affection for her – making breakfast for her, inviting her to a concert or fixing the tap in her bathroom – as a manifestation of love, and she ended up believing that he was in love with her although he was unwilling to recognize it.

As in the example of the workmates considered at the beginning, it is easy to see that this situation resembles to some extent a situation in which the belief is justified because the evidence is good enough. If our friend had behaved differently with one of these women – remaining with her after breakfast, asking her to spend the summer together or introducing her to his mother – it would have been reasonable for her to believe that he was in love with her. But he did not do any such thing, and it is very unlikely that what prevented him from doing them was his unwillingness to recognize his love.

3.3 Evidence without belief

The second effect of wishful thinking is that one may not believe that p, because one desires that it not be the case that p, even though one has enough evidence for believing that p. Instead of believing things that are far from obvious, as in the cases considered in the previous section, one may fail to believe things that are obvious.

Sometimes lovers are reluctant to accept obvious truths that conflict with their expectations. A friend of one of us was so firmly convinced of the faithfulness of her boyfriend, that when she found women's lingerie in his bedroom – and it happened more than once – she believed the boyfriend's story that the lingerie belonged to his sister, who visited him quite often and was a little messy. In spite of the fact that she had unequivocal evidence for believing that her boyfriend was cheating on her, she refused to believe this, and believed the opposite instead.

This second effect of wishful thinking is often combined with the first. It may happen that one believes that p without having good evidence for believing that p and having instead good evidence for believing that it is not the case that p. In other words, one may believe that p in the absence of good positive evidence and in the presence of good negative evidence. Most of the time, when lovers have unjustified beliefs based on wishful thinking, they tend to make both mistakes: on the one hand, they overestimate the positive evidence; on the other, they underestimate the negative evidence. The following example shows this combination of effects:

> Alex and Kiko are having an affair. They meet in parks, motels, and restaurants, because Kiko is married and has two children. After a year of secret dates and passionate sex, Alex asks Kiko if she intends to leave her family to be with him. Kiko reassures him and says that she would do anything for him. But time goes by and nothing happens. Alex asks again more vehemently, and Kiko reassures him again. The situation does not change, and conversations of this kind occur with increasing regularity. Nonetheless, Alex is convinced that one day Kiko will divorce: if she has not done so yet, it is just a matter of time.

In this case, Alex has an unjustified belief based on wishful thinking, the belief that Kiko will divorce. What makes it unjustified is neither a total absence of positive evidence nor a substantial body of negative evidence. Some facts – her declarations of love, her passionate kisses and so on – may suggest that she will divorce, while others – her broken promises, the problems that she would have to face and so on – may suggest that she will not divorce. The problem is that he attaches too much importance to facts of the first kind and too little to those of the second kind.

Some cases of this kind grow into extreme situations in which the self-deception fostered by wishful thinking causes pathological forms of misperception. Psychologist Stephen Grosz tells the story of a patient of his, call her Helen, who spent nine years having an affair with a married colleague, call him Robert. Blinded by her morbid love, Helen was unable to see facts that were in front of her eyes. In nine years, Robert never kept his promises. Once he promised to spend his vacation with her, but eventually he left with his wife. Another time he promised to divorce and asked her to wait until his son went to college, but when the moment came he did not divorce. One day, Robert told her that he had met another woman and that he was going to leave his wife to be with her. Instead of recognizing that Robert was in love with that woman and not with her, Helen told Grosz that she knew what was going to happen, that this proved, against her friends, that Robert was capable of leaving his wife, and concluded that Robert's new lover certainly did not know how to take care of him, so he was going to return to her. Of course, this was a possibility, albeit a quite remote one, but Helen took it to be a certainty.

So far, we have considered cases in which two persons are involved in a relationship and one of them has unjustified beliefs based on wishful thinking. But it may also happen that both the persons involved in a relationship have such beliefs. A quite familiar situation is that in which two persons live a tormented love story marked by regular and intense crises, each of which looks like a prelude to a definitive breakup. Immediately after each crisis, they say to their respective friends 'It's over', 'I knew it couldn't last' or 'This time is different, there is no way back', even though after a while the two lovers see each other again as if nothing had happened. The fact is that when they say such things to their friends, they really believe what they say, and probably they believe such things because in that moment they desire what they say to be true. But their beliefs are unjustified, for their record of crises and reconciliations suggests the opposite of what they believe. Of course, for each crisis, it is possible that their beliefs about that particular crisis are true, namely, that there will be no reconciliation after that crisis. But this does not mean that their beliefs about that particular crisis are justified, for their experience of previous crises provides no reason to rule out that they will once again make up. If they believe that there will be no reconciliation after that crisis, it is because in that moment they desire it.

3.4 Love is blind

To conclude our outline of the misperceptions of reality caused by desire, we shall dwell on a psychological phenomenon that is analogous to wishful thinking but that concerns perception rather than belief. This phenomenon, which may be called *wishful seeing*, is the tendency to see what one desires. Just as one can believe that p because one desires that p, one can see that p because one desires that p. Similarly, just as one can fail to believe that p because one desires that it not be the case that p, one can fail to see that p because one desires that it not be the case that p. Here, the already mentioned metaphor of the glasses is even more fitting.

The first form of wishful seeing is very common. Generally, the lover sees in the beloved features that the lover or others judge positively. For example, when a man loves a thin woman, he may see in her the slim figure of a top model, while his friends simply see her as a thin woman.

The second form of wishful seeing is also very common. Generally, the lover does not see in the beloved features that the lover or others judge negatively. For example, when a woman loves a short man, she may see him as a little taller than he really is, while her friends simply see him as a short man.

Note that a case of wishful seeing must not be confused with one in which the lover recognizes the absence of some positive feature, or the presence of some negative feature, but intentionally disregards these as immaterial. As long as the lover's perception of the beloved is correct, there is no cognitive mistake. It is one thing to know that your beloved is 1.55 metres and pay little attention to height and quite another thing to think that he is about 10 centimetres taller than he really is.

The features that lovers see, or fail to see, in their beloved may heavily depend on the standards of beauty that hold in their society. If a man sees his beloved as being as slim as a top model, it is very likely because he lives in a society where slim women are preferred to curvy women. Another man, who lives in a society where curvy women are preferred to slim women, will be apt to see his beloved as more curvy than she really is. Therefore, the properties that lovers see, or fail to see, in their beloved may vary widely from society to society. Note, however, that such differences are inessential to the definition of wishful seeing. This illustrates clearly the point made in Section 1.6 that the existence of cultural divergences does not entail variation at the epistemological level. Even if the first man sees his beloved as slim while the second sees his beloved as curvy, their cognitive mistake is exactly the same.

What we have said about wishful seeing can be generalized in at least three directions. The first concerns the effects of wishful seeing on persons other than the beloved. So far, we have talked about the visual distortions that affect the lover's perception of the beloved, but it is easy to see that similar distortions may affect a lover's perception of other people. Typically, when the lover considers potential rivals of the beloved, that is, other persons in the same range of sex, age, education and so on, he or she is naturally apt to pay more attention to the negative features of those persons and less attention to their positive features.[2]

The second generalization concerns the senses other than sight. Our use of the expression 'wishful seeing' is not intended to suggest that sight is the only sense that can be affected by the kind of distortions considered. Although the case of sight is particularly interesting, the same kind of distortions can affect other senses. For example, the skin of the beloved may seem to the lover softer than it actually is, and the voice of the beloved may seem to the lover less shrill than it actually is. In general, one can perceive that p because one desires that p, and one can fail to perceive that p because one desires that it not be the case that p.

The third generalization concerns the features of the beloved that are not literally perceived. It is plausible that distortions similar to those considered can go beyond the five senses, namely, that they can affect the perception of the beloved in a broader sense of 'perception'. An experience that has happened to us many times is that in which we hear a person telling jokes and anecdotes that are not particularly amusing but that cause great laughter in another person who finds the first person attractive. In a situation of this kind, the second person perceives as funny something that others – like us – do not perceive as funny. Probably, the same jokes and anecdotes would not seem equally funny to that person if they were told by someone else.

3.5 The diamond fallacy

The last fallacy that we shall consider, the *diamond fallacy*, is similar to the other fallacies presented so far in that it implies a distorted perception of reality. Yet it differs from those fallacies in one important respect. Instead of believing without justification that things are better than they actually are, in this case the lover believes without justification that things are worse than they actually are. More precisely, one commits the diamond fallacy when one thinks that the loved person does not return one's love, or is not committed enough, because that person does not do something that one regards as an indispensable manifestation of love. The name of the fallacy comes from the commonplace that a diamond is the best proof of love. According to this commonplace, if your boyfriend does not buy you a diamond ring, he does not 'really' love you.[3]

In order to spell out this fallacy it will help to focus on a specific example. Suppose that Alex and Kiko are boyfriend and girlfriend, and that one day Kiko tells Alex: 'You don't love me, you never buy me flowers!' Even if it is true that Alex never buys flowers for Kiko, she does not have any justification for believing that he does not love her. Flowers are generally regarded as a sign of love: if one buys flowers for a person, it is because one loves that person. However, the converse does not hold. Love without flowers is possible. For example, a friend of one of us (another friend, not the one mentioned in Section 3.2) does not give flowers to the woman he loves because he sees flowers as a trick that men use when they try to impress women or make amends for their misdeeds. Thus, although it may be true that if Alex buys flowers for Kiko, then he loves her, from this it does not follow that if Alex does not buy flowers for Kiko, then he does not love her.

Note that this is not the only admissible reading of Kiko's words. Perhaps Kiko is not so simple-minded as to think that Alex does not love her just because of the lack of flowers. Perhaps if Alex objected that some lovers never give flowers, Kiko would reply that the problem is not just the flowers: he never takes her out for a romantic dinner, he never gives her any gifts and so on. That is, on a more charitable reading of Kiko's words, she means something like 'You don't love me because you never do those things, such as giving me flowers, which would show that you love me.' In other words, Kiko is saying that Alex does not perform any of the actions it is natural to expect from a loving boyfriend. Of course, she might be right if he is completely inattentive.

However, Kiko could be wrong even in such a case. Different persons may have different ideas about what actions count as proper manifestations of love. Kiko might believe that Alex does not love her simply because he does not perform any of the actions that *she* takes to be proper manifestations of love, even though he does perform all the actions that *he* takes to be proper manifestations of love. This kind of misunderstanding is quite frequent. When two persons are involved in a love relationship, each of them expresses his or her love in some specific way, and usually expects the other to express his or her love in the same way, so they have problems when their expectations differ.

One last remark. We have seen that the diamond fallacy differs from the previous fallacies in that the lover believes without justification that things are worse than they actually are. The lover's belief is not consolatory in this case, for there is nothing consolatory in the thought that your beloved does not love you. Therefore, the unjustified belief is not driven by desire. Note, however, that desire is not the only possible source of alterations in the perception of reality. Another possible source is fear. If you are swimming in the ocean and you see a dark thing shaped like a triangle bobbing up and down in the middle of the waves, you may easily think that it is the dorsal fin of a shark, even if the dorsal fin of a dolphin or the head of sea turtle would look exactly the same from your position. What makes you think that it is a shark is that you are afraid of sharks. Similarly, the lover may be apt to think that something of which he or she is afraid – not being loved – is more likely than something else. Robinson Crusoe, we may recall, is afraid of the devil when he entertains his first unpleasant hypothesis.

4

Wanting it all

L'amour c'est être stupide ensemble.

P. VALERY[1]

4.1 Complex cases of cognitive mistakes

The fallacies considered in Chapters 2 and 3 are simple cases of cognitive mistakes, that is, cases in which one person has a single unjustified belief. We illustrated these fallacies one by one in order to spell out their essential features. But in real life it almost never happens that a love situation that involves two persons is describable in terms of a single unjustified belief held by one of them. The most common cases are instead complex cases of cognitive mistakes, that is, cases in which the interaction between two persons produces forms of self-deception based on the reiteration of a single fallacy or on the combination of different fallacies. In this chapter, we shall consider four complex cases of cognitive mistakes, which constitute paradigmatic love situations.

Although each of these four cases exhibits distinctive features that make it easily identifiable, there is an important trait in common to all of them. Any minimally stable love relationship requires that one gives up some expectations and accepts some compromises. So there are essentially three attitudes that one can have towards such a relationship: one commits oneself to the relationship and accepts its unwanted consequences, or one does not commit oneself to the relationship just because one is unwilling to accept its undesirable consequences, or one tries to have the relationship without accepting its undesirable consequences. The common trait of the cases that we shall consider is the presence of this third attitude. In each of them, one of the two persons involved *wants it all*, so to say.

One thing that must be noted about these four cases is that many interesting questions that arise in connection with them fall outside the scope of our investigation. In particular, we will not deal with any moral questions. Although it might be asked whether or to what extent it is morally admissible to be in a love relation without accepting its undesirable consequences, we will not address this question. Similarly, we will not talk about the moral implications that depend on the distinctive features of each case. This book, unlike other philosophy books on love, is not a book of moral philosophy. As far as we are concerned, the only thing that matters about the characters we will describe is their cognitive profile, and more precisely their unjustified beliefs.

Another thing that must be noted about these four cases is that the choice of the characters that we will describe is not intended to suggest correlations between differences of sex or gender and types of cognitive mistakes. As we said in Section 1.5, we are interested in the mistakes themselves, rather than in who commits them. Some of the characters will be men, others will be women. But this essentially depends on the literary sources that we adopt. In reality, in each of the four cases, the cognitive role played by each character can equally be instantiated by men or women, or by males or females.

4.2 The Divided Lover

The first character that we shall consider, *the Divided Lover*, is drawn from an old Cuban song: 'Corazón Loco' by A. Machín. This song is about a man who explains how can he love two women at the same time without going crazy (the title of the song means 'Crazy Heart'). The explanation is that one of the two women, his wife, is 'the sacred love', 'mate of his life' and 'spouse and mother at once', while the other, his mistress, is 'the forbidden love', 'soother of his anxieties' and 'whom he'll not give up'. In other words, the man wants to have both the serenity of a stable relationship and the excitement of a passionate affair. His wife and his mistress play different emotional roles, so to say, and he believes that one and the same person could not play both roles.

In order to grasp the essence of the Divided Lover, it is important to understand that some details of this story are totally irrelevant. First, it is irrelevant that our character is a man, that for him it is fine to have a mistress in addition to a wife, or any other implication of the 'machista' cliché that permeates the song. All that matters here is that the Divided Lover loves two persons and has certain beliefs about them. Note that the characterization of love suggested in Section 1.1 is consistent with the possibility of loving different persons at the same time. Second, although our man may cheat on his wife, as she may be unaware of his affair, we will not regard this as an essential trait of the Divided Lover. As far as we are concerned, he may equally have an honest relationship with the two women instead of cheating on his wife. Third, what we will say about the Divided Lover can easily be extended to different or more complex situations. Instead of a triangle that involves one man and two women, there can be different triangles, or more complex geometrical figures. If 'polyamory' is used as a general term for non-monogamous love relationships, our account of the Divided Lover can be applied to cases of polyamory.

The distinctive feature of the Divided Lover as we understand him is that he is attracted to two distinct emotional roles played by his wife and by his mistress. He regards both as desirable, but thinks that they are not realizable in the same person. He loves his wife in virtue of properties that according to him make her a good wife, and he loves his mistress in virtue of properties that according to him make her a good mistress. In other words, he does not love each of the two women as the person she is, but as the person that instantiates a certain role. This is not itself wrong from an epistemological point of view. But it leads the Divided Lover to form an unjustified belief, the belief that each of the two women, besides having some properties that makes her suitable for the role she actually plays, lacks other properties that would make her suitable for the other role. According to him, one is ideal as a wife, the other is ideal as a mistress, and neither of them could do equally well what the other does.

As we have said, this is the Divided Lover as we define him. We do not intend to suggest that any person involved in a situation of the type described has such a belief. Thus, we will not consider the case in which a man simply believes that one and the same woman cannot play *simultaneously* the role of the wife and the role of the mistress, for that belief may be justified. More generally, we will not consider cases in which a polyamorous person loves two or more persons without having unjustified beliefs about them.

To see that the belief of the Divided Lover is unjustified it is important to note that the properties that he values may be identified with dispositions: to be a good wife, or a good mistress, is to be disposed to do certain things in certain circumstances. Because his wife does certain things (she has breakfast with him every day, she takes care of their children, and so on), he believes that she is a good wife. Because his mistress does certain things (she loves him in a passionate way, she listens to him when he talks about his secret dreams, and so on), he believes that she is a good mistress. So far there is nothing wrong, because these beliefs may be justified. But the Divided Lover also thinks that neither of the two women can play the role of the other, and this belief is not justified, at least if it is based on the mere fact that in actual circumstances the two women do not display the relevant properties. Each of them might have properties that characterize the other, even though these properties are not actually manifested. As noted in Section 1.1, one can have a disposition even if one does not manifest it in certain circumstances.

Note that the belief of the Divided Lover might be true. It might be the case that each of the two women really is unable to play the role of the other. But this does not make it justified. It is also possible that the two women have very similar properties, but that each of them manifests only some of her properties because of the role she actually plays. For example, if the woman who is actually his wife were not married to him, she could be the passionate mistress of another man (maybe she actually is the passionate mistress of another man). Similarly, the woman who is actually his mistress could be the lovely wife of someone else.

The cognitive flaw of the Divided Lover becomes clear if we imagine what would happen if he decided to leave his wife to be with his mistress. In that case, his mistress would end up playing the role of his wife, or at least this is a possible scenario. So, he could either stop being Divided or find another mistress. In the second case, he would probably start seeing the second mistress as the ideal mistress and the first mistress as the ideal wife. But this evidently clashes with the fact that he himself regarded the first mistress as the ideal mistress, when she was his mistress. At any one time, the Divided Lover thinks that the woman who plays a given role at that time is ideal for that role. In other words, what makes him believe that a person, in certain circumstances, is suitable for a given role, and unsuitable for another, is simply that the person actually plays only that role in those circumstances.

4.3 The Princess

Everybody knows how the story of Cinderella ends:

First she washed her face and hands quite clean, and went in and curtseyed to the Prince, who held out to her the golden shoe. Then she sat down on a stool, drew her foot out of the heavy wooden shoe, and slipped it into the golden one, which fitted it perfectly. And when she stood up, and the Prince looked in her face, he knew again the beautiful maiden that had danced with him, and he cried, 'This is the right bride!' The step-mother and the two sisters were thunderstruck, and grew pale with anger; but he put Cinderella before him on his horse and rode off.

J. GRIMM AND W. GRIMM, *Cinderella*

In the end, everything goes well for Cinderella (or at least, it goes well for Cinderella according to the authors of *Cinderella*): Prince Charming comes and saves her. But such things happen only in fairy tales. In real life Prince Charming never shows up, simply because he does not exist. Real men are definitely not like him. They are less noble, less virtuous, less handsome and above all they do not make every effort to find a girl they met at a party if the only clue they have is a shoe. Nonetheless, some people behave as if Prince Charming existed. The second character that we shall consider, *the Princess*, is defined by this kind of behaviour. The Princess is a person who behaves as if Prince Charming existed, that is, as if somebody could satisfy all of her desires.

The Princess clearly differs from the Divided Lover. The Divided Lover thinks that no single person can satisfy all of his desires, so he seeks to satisfy different desires with different persons. The Princess, instead, is unwilling to accept that no single person can satisfy all of her desires. She seems to think that, somewhere, there is somebody who can give her everything she wants, namely, Prince Charming. Of course, she recognizes that it may be very hard to find him. After all, you cannot expect a man with such uncommon qualities to be waiting for you just around the corner. But if you seek carefully, and you have patience, you may be lucky. Since the Princess always has Prince Charming in her mind, her love relationships follow a recurrent pattern: they begin full of hope and eagerness ('It might be him'), then they go through a period of trials and examinations ('Is it really him?'), until the sad and disappointing epilogue comes round ('It was not him'). Her desire to find the man of her dreams is thus constantly hindered by her own expectations, which cannot be met.

The profile just described is compatible with at least three different cases. In the first case, the Princess believes that Prince Charming exists because she is socialized into believing that he exists. As a result of her upbringing, and of massive amounts of telenovelas and romantic comedies, the Princess is inclined to expect that there really are men like Prince Charming, so that the best she can do is wait for such a man to show up and choose her. In this case, the Princess certainly has an unjustified belief, for there is no reason to think that there are men like Prince

Charming. But she does not commit any interesting cognitive mistake, for her belief is like any other unjustified belief induced by the social environment.[2]

In the second case, the Princess believes that Prince Charming exists because she desires him to exist, as she would like to be with a perfect man. In this case, the Princess has fallen into wishful thinking. Although there is nothing irrational in her desire – after all, she is not the only one who would like to be with a perfect man – her belief is unjustified. There is no reason to think that Prince Charming exists. If she believes that Prince Charming exists, it is only because she desires it.

The first and the second case may easily combine to form a mixed case. On the one hand, if the Princess is socialized into believing that Prince Charming exists, it is very likely that she desires to be with him, so she will be apt to strengthen her belief through wishful thinking. On the other, if the Princess believes that Prince Charming exists because she desires to be with him, it may happen that her belief finds further support in the ideals and in the models of behaviour that permeate her society.

The third case is significantly different. In this case, the Princess believes that Prince Charming exists without really desiring to be with him. The belief that Prince Charming exists helps her to rationalize a fact that she is reluctant to accept, namely, the fact that she does not want to be with anyone. The

Princess tells herself, and repeats to her friends, that she would like to be with someone. But she rejects all the men she actually meets, and motivates her rejection by measuring those men against impossibly high standards. With such standards, only Prince Charming would pass the test. In other words, Prince Charming is the excuse she adopts to explain the failure of her relationships. Her cognitive mistake, therefore, is an inference to the worst explanation. Instead of recognizing that she is alone because she wants to be alone, she looks for alternative explanations that make her feel better.

In each of the three cases considered, the Princess believes without justification that Prince Charming exists. Note, however, that in none of them is it essential that the Princess acknowledges her belief. Certainly, if the Princess is sufficiently gullible, she may openly endorse the claim that there are men like Prince Charming. But it may also happen that she is unwilling to commit herself to that claim, and consequently that she fails to acknowledge her belief. As we saw in Section 1.4, one may be wrong about one's own mental states. So the Princess may believe that Prince Charming exists without believing that she believes that Prince Charming exists, or even believing that she does not believe that Prince Charming exists. Moreover, in the third case, the Princess may also have an unjustified second-order belief about her desires. That is, she may believe that she desires that Prince Charming exists and that she wants to be with him, whereas in reality she does not have such a desire at all.

The unjustified belief that Prince Charming exists can have negative consequences for the Princess. The most striking effect of this belief, as we have seen, is that it leads the Princess to reject all the men she actually meets, thus increasing her chances of remaining alone. In the first two cases considered this is a serious problem for the Princess, because she does not want to be alone. Probably, if she did not believe that Prince Charming exists, she would regard some of the men she actually rejects as sufficiently good candidates.

Other effects of the belief that Prince Charming exists, which are less tangible but no less insidious, concern the ways in which the Princess behaves *during* her relationships. In each of the three cases considered, the Princess can spend months or even years with a real partner. But her constant tendency to compare her partner with Prince Charming causes unnecessary troubles that inevitably affect her relationship with him. For example, in certain circumstances she may feel sad or disappointed if he does not act in a particularly attentive or romantic way with her, even though she does not act in that way with him. In those circumstances, she may easily think that he does not love her enough, as in the diamond fallacy, simply because he does not love her as Prince Charming would love her.

4.4 The Don Juan

Madamina, il catalogo è questo

Delle belle che amò il padron mio;

un catalogo egli è che ho fatt'io:

osservate, leggete con me.

In Italia seicento e quaranta,

in Lamagna duecento e trentuna,

cento in Francia, in Turchia novantuna,

ma in Ispagna son già mille e tre.

V'ha fra queste contadine,

cameriere, cittadine,

v'han contesse, baronesse,

e v'han donne d'ogni grado,

d'ogni forma, d'ogni età.[3]

L. DA PONTE, *Don Giovanni*

The third kind of want-it-all attitude characterizes the persons who tend to have as many love relationships as they can. Very often, these persons are moved by the desire to live an indefinite number of times the moment of seduction, which is a distinctively intense and exciting stage of a love story. Since it is impossible to live this moment forever with the same person, the only way to experience it again and again is to live it with different persons. Another desire that may drive these persons to change their partners incessantly is the desire of the collector, because they find pleasure in the amount and in the variety of their conquests. Finally, these persons may enjoy the satisfaction of testing their power over other people. In any case, we will not speculate about the deep psychological causes of their inclinations, for what matters for our purposes is their behaviour.

The figure that best epitomizes the attitude just described is Don Juan, the legendary and dissolute Spanish nobleman who became famous for his ability as a seducer. The fame of Don Juan is due to several literary and musical works in which he features as a character, such as the opera by Mozart cited above. We will not go through the details of the character as it appears in these works, and we will not consider the interesting philosophical questions that may be raised, and that have been raised, in connection with it. For present purposes it will suffice to consider a type of situation, call it a *Don Juan situation*, that involves two persons – *the Don Juan* and *the Victim* – who resemble Don Juan and one of his numerous victims.

An essential feature of a Don Juan situation as we understand it is that the Don Juan behaves as if he were in love with the Victim, and as a consequence of this the Victim believes that he is in love with her. In the following verses, Don Juan flatters Inés with the help of eloquent metaphors:

esta llama que en mi mismo
se alimenta inextinguible,

va creciendo y más voraz

…

En vano a apagarla

concurren tiempo y ausencia

que doblando su violencia,

no hoguera ya, volcán es.

Y yo, que en medio del cráter

desamparado batallo,

suspendido en él me hallo

entre mi tumba y mi Inés.

…

Inés, alma de mi alma,

perpetuo imán de mi vida,

perla sin concha escondida

entre las algas del mar.[4]

J. ZORRILLA, *Don Juan Tenorio*

To say that the Don Juan behaves as if he were in love with the Victim is not quite the same thing as to say that he lies to the Victim. It may be the case that the Don Juan behaves the way he does because he is really convinced that he loves the Victim, even if his conviction then evaporates quite rapidly. In any case, no matter whether the Don Juan believes this or not, it is essential that the Victim believes that he is in love with her, for the success of the Don Juan depends at least in part on the fact that he induces the Victim to believe in his love. In this respect, the Don Juan differs from an ordinary womanizer who is not particularly interested in the game of romance. The success of such a person may depend simply on sex appeal, conversational skills or money, with no intention to convince the other person that he is in love with her.

Let us examine a Don Juan situation from an epistemological point of view. First of all the Don Juan does not commit any specific cognitive mistake. He desires the Victim to fall in love with him, he is justified in believing that, if he behaves in a certain way, he is very likely to get the desired result, so he acts in accordance with his desire and his belief. Of course, the Don Juan might also believe – for a short time – that he is in love with the Victim, and this additional belief could be unjustified. But we have seen that it is not essential that the Don Juan believes that he is in love with the Victim, for all that matters is that he behaves as if he were. If the Don Juan does not believe that he is in love with the Victim, his cognitive profile is perfectly rational.

Obviously, to say that the Don Juan behaves impeccably from an epistemological point of view is not to say that, from the psychological point of view, all is well with him. Perhaps there is something pathological about his behaviour. However, as we have said, we will not talk about the deep psychological causes of his inclinations. Similarly, to say that the Don Juan is impeccable from an epistemological point of view is not to say that he is blameless from the moral point of view. After all, he deceives the Victim by overemphasizing his love dispositions or by simulating love dispositions that he does not have. But again, we will not address moral questions, and we are primarily interested in self-deception rather than in ordinary deception.

Now let us consider the Victim. Unlike the Don Juan, the Victim has unjustified beliefs: she believes that the Don Juan is in love with her, that he wants to be with her, and so on. Certainly, these unjustified beliefs depend at least in part on the fact that the Don Juan deceives her, and she cannot be blamed for that. But the Victim also deceives herself, because she tends to underestimate the negative evidence she has, namely, the fact that the Don Juan has conquered and abandoned many other women before. Here we are assuming that the Don Juan has a certain reputation, and that the Victim knows who he is.

As in the case of the affair considered in Section 3.3, the Victim falls into the trap of wishful thinking. All things considered, she should not believe – except perhaps at the very beginning of the relationship – that the Don Juan is in love with her, that he wants to be with her, and so on. The record of his past experiences provides strong evidence against those beliefs, even though sometimes his behaviour may suggest otherwise. If she believes that the Don Juan is in love with her, that he wants to be with her, and so on, it is only because she desires such things.

The effect of wishful thinking is often combined with some forms of rationalization. The Victim may be apt to rationalize her beliefs by thinking things such as 'With me it will be different' or 'He will change', as in *The Seducer's Diary* by Søren Kierkegaard. This book tells the story of Johannes, who stealthily pursues the innocent Cordelia until she becomes increasingly drawn to him. As soon as they are engaged, Johannes schemes to have her question their engagement by becoming distant and allowing her to pursue him. When she perceives his distance from her, her passion increases and she convinces herself that he will change and will love her again as before.

That you did love me, I know, even though I do not know what it is that makes me sure of it. I will wait, however long the time is for me; I will wait, wait until you are tired of loving others. Then your love for me will rise again from its grave; then I will love you as always, thank you as always, as before, O Johannes, as before! Johannes, is your heartless coldness toward me, is it your true nature? Was your love, your rich love, a lie and a falsehood; are you now yourself gain! Have patience with my love; forgive me for continuing to love you. I know that my love is a burden to you, but there will still come a time when you will come back to your Cordelia.

S. KIERKEGAARD, *The Seducer's Diary*

4.5 The emotional terrorizer

The last case that we shall consider is definitely the most complex from the cognitive point of view and the most destructive from the emotional point of view. The kind of behaviour that we will describe is represented very clearly in *El perro del hortelano* by Félix Lope de Vega. The title of this comedy, translated in English as *The Dog in the Manger*, is a metaphor that comes from a Greek fable. There are several versions of the fable, but in most of them a dog won't let another animal eat some food that he himself cannot or will not eat. The metaphor is used to speak of those who spitefully prevent others from having something that they themselves have no use for. In the comedy, the haughty countess Diana falls in love with her handsome young secretary, Teodoro, who is the lover of her maid Marcela. Unwilling to let the couple marry, she is also unwilling to marry him herself. The story of Diana and Teodoro illustrates the type of situation that we will consider. When Teodoro is rejected by Diana, after experiencing her passionate love, he talks to his friend Tristán and says that he does not know what to think:

> No sé, Tristán; pierdo el seso
> de ver que me está adorando,
> y que me aborrece luego.
> No quiere que sea suyo

ni de Marcela; y si dejo

de mirarla, luego busca

por hablarme algún enredo.

No dudes: naturalmente

es del hortelano el perro.

Ni come ni comer deja,

ni está fuera ni está dentro.[5]

F. LOPE DE VEGA, *El perro del hortelano*

This is what Teodoro says to Diana:

Tan poco

que te siento y no te entiendo

pues no entiendo tus palabras,

y tus bofetones siento.

Si no te quiero te enfadas,

y enójaste si te quiero;

escríbesme si me olvido,

y si me acuerdo te ofendo;

pretendes que yo te entienda,

y si te entiendo soy necio.

Mátame o dame la vida;

da un medio a tantos extremos.[6]

F. LOPE DE VEGA, *El perro del hortelano*

Diana and Teodoro exemplify in a paradigmatic way the kind of behaviour that we will call *emotional terrorism*, because Diana emotionally terrorizes Teodoro. From now on, taking inspiration from these two characters, we will talk generically about *the Terrorizer* and *the Terrorized*.

We are all familiar with situations in which two persons are involved in a love relationship and one of them likes being pursued by the other, running away when the other tries to get closer and returning when the other withdraws. Within certain limits, this is a common strategy of seduction. Or at least, if used with moderation, together with other strategies, it is one of the ingredients of seduction. But when it acquires a dominant role and becomes the leitmotif of a love story, then it is emotional terrorism. Just like the dog in the manger, the Terrorizer keeps the Terrorized suspended in a state in which he is neither loved by her as he wishes nor capable of loving someone else. The distinctive form of interaction that develops between the Terrorizer and the Terrorized arises when, after being rejected by the Terrorizer, the Terrorized tries to walk away, the Terrorizer goes back and pursues him until she manages to reconquer him. Once he surrenders, she rejects him again and so on. This process can occur several times, so the relationship can last for months, even years. As long as the story lasts, the Terrorized will increasingly lose his confidence in the Terrorizer's promises, and the Terrorizer, in order to overcome resistance, will insist with increasingly strong manifestations of love. For example, she will show sadness when the Terrorized is not with her, joy when he resists the temptation to walk away and so on. This way she will be able to win again and again.

The Terrorizer exhibits a special kind of want-it-all attitude. On the one hand, she wants all of the Terrorized. She constantly exerts her influence on him, pushing his endurance to the limit. The fact that he shows increasingly less confidence in her promises makes the game increasingly more challenging for her. Her capacity to triumph over the resistance of the Terrorized over and over again gives her the sensation of overcoming an apparently infinite series of obstacles, satisfying and titillating her desire to dominate the situation. On the other hand, she does not want to maintain her possession of the Terrorized uninterruptedly. She wants to have him, loose him, win him back and so on. Neither of the two conditions satisfies her completely. Perhaps what satisfies her is the transition from the one to the other or the oscillation between them, and, of course, the prospect that the transitions and oscillations will continue.

An essential feature of emotional terrorism as we understand it is that the Terrorizer, at least to some degree, believes that she loves the Terrorized. Certainly, the Terrorizer is well aware that sometimes she deliberately turns away from the Terrorized. But she believes that she has reasons for doing so. For example, she may believe that she is forced to turn him away because she is committed to someone else, or because she has just emerged from a very difficult love story and needs time to reflect, or because her job is too demanding, or because she does not feel 'ready' to commit herself to a serious relationship, or even – she can be so far gone – because the love she feels is so great that she does not want to 'lessen' or 'constrain' it within the bounds of an ordinary relationship.

Note that the motivations provided by the Terrorizer may be well grounded: she may have real problems. But the fact is that she uses her problems as excuses, so she does nothing to overcome them. In a way, problems are fine for her. If one of her problems disappears, she will immediately find another, so that the Terrorized will keep pursuing her. This is why the interaction between the Terrorizer and the Terrorized is characterized by a sequence of pursuits, rejections, reconciliations, advances and retreats, which ensure that the tension within the couple never lessens and always increases.

From the psychological point of view, the Terrorizer and the Terrorized are both anomalous to some extent. On the one hand, the Terrorizer finds pleasure only in the possession and in the manipulation of the Terrorized, and seeks satisfaction in the challenges caused by his increasing resistance. On the other, the Terrorized is trapped in a state of addiction that resembles drug dependency, because, in spite of his deep and constant agony, which can sometimes drive him crazy, he gets from his interaction with the Terrorizer some emotional reward that prevents him from escaping. This situation produces a mental trap that keeps him under the control of the Terrorizer. Again, we will not speculate on the deep psychological causes of these inclinations. Our goal is to identify the unjustified beliefs that characterize emotional terrorism.

In contrast to a Don Juan situation, emotional terrorism is a situation where the irrationality may be present on both sides. Both the Terrorizer and the Terrorized may have unjustified beliefs, and they may both deceive themselves. First let us consider the Terrorizer. Clearly, she has justified beliefs: she believes that the Terrorized loves her, that if she behaves in certain ways then she will get certain results and so on. But she also has unjustified beliefs. She may believe that she truly loves the Terrorized, without having a justification for believing so. Although she manifests some love dispositions in some crucial moments, she does not really behave like a lover. First, the love dispositions she manifests are not constant, for they appear only when she needs them to pursue and reconquer the Terrorized. Second, she lacks some characteristic love dispositions, such as the disposition to accept actions that go against her interests. Third, she manifests dispositions that typically do not belong to lovers, such as the disposition to walk away just when the relationship starts working.

Although this lack of love dispositions provides clear reasons to doubt that the Terrorizer loves the Terrorized, the Terrorizer herself may firmly believe that she loves the Terrorized. Her inclination to believe so is likely to derive from two desires: one is the desire that the belief itself be true, because she would like to love him, the other is the desire to regain something lost, because in certain moments she feels and regrets that he is no longer there. This is to say that her misrepresentation of herself is due to wishful thinking and to the lost love fallacy. Note that the form of wishful thinking involved here is particularly perverse. The Terrorizer believes that she loves the Terrorized because she would like to love him, but she does not desire to live with him in a stable relationship based on reciprocal love, as in normal cases of wishful thinking.

The Terrorizer may also be subject to the effects of rationalization. Since she is aware that a considerable part of her behaviour does not match her belief that she loves the Terrorized, she is inclined to explain that part of her behaviour by appealing to problems that would hinder her relationship with him and so would prevent her from manifesting all her love. Of course, these problems may be real, as noted above. But she uses them as excuses to justify her behaviour, so they are not the real cause of her lack of love.

Now let us consider the Terrorized. The Terrorized, just like the Terrorizer, believes both that he loves the Terrorizer and that the Terrorizer loves him. The first belief is justified, while the second is unjustified. So the main difference between the Terrorizer and the Terrorized is that while she is right about him but wrong about herself, he is right about himself but wrong about her. Their epistemological profiles are somehow complementary.

Perhaps at the beginning of the story the Terrorized may have some positive evidence and no negative evidence for believing that the Terrorizer loves him. But, as the plot unfolds, the negative evidence constantly grows until it overwhelms the positive evidence. As we have said, some positive evidence is always there: the Terrorizer manifests some love dispositions from time to time, she keeps saying that she loves him and so on. But when he acquires a substantial body of negative evidence, he should abandon his belief. If he still believes that she loves him, it is only because he desires this to be the case. So the Terrorized, like the Terrorizer, is guilty of wishful thinking.

The Terrorized is also a victim of another form of self-deception, one that typically affects drug addicts. Not only does he believe, when he is with the Terrorizer, that she loves him, but he also believes, when he decides to walk away, that he is no longer in her power. In the moments in which he feels that he has distanced himself enough from her, the Terrorized may think 'It's over. I'm not going to see her again', 'If she shows up again, I will not allow her to play with me' or 'Now I'm out of it. From now on I can see her only as a friend.' However, he has no reasons for believing such things, because his past experience suggests that all his attempts to free himself from her have failed miserably. Again, if he believes such things, it is only because in those moments he desires them.

A long time ago, when this book was just a project, a friend of one of us explained that he had just broken off a long relationship with a woman who fits the profile of the Terrorizer. He said that he was finally free from her and was quite clear that she was not going to come back ever again. As his words produced a sceptical reaction, he promised to keep us posted about future developments. After some months, just when we were working on this section, he showed up again and confessed that he and his lover were back together and that now everything was fine. Just as before, he was firmly convinced that the terrorist dialectic was over, that the situation was under control. Unfortunately, however, things did not go as he expected. Some weeks later he admitted that he had once again fallen into her trap, and was once again suffering as before.

The Terrorizer comes back, but never as a friend. So the Terrorized may easily surrender to her, and deceive himself as before. The strength of his illusion that she loves him increases all the time in order to deal with all the new evidence against the belief that she loves him. The same goes for his illusion that he can escape. It is a cognitively dramatic situation, because the strength of each unjustified belief must overcome the negative evidence that supports the previous unjustified belief. So he finds himself in a spiral of self-deception, where unjustified beliefs are constantly replaced by unjustified beliefs, and the strength of his beliefs continues to increase. This generates a feeling of being trapped, as when one is in a tunnel and can see no way out. As a result, the Terrorized may suffer sorely and lose self-esteem, which in turn fosters his need for rationalization and wishful thinking.

What makes the situation extremely complex is the interaction between the Terrorizer and the Terrorized. The Terrorized needs constantly to increase the strength of his beliefs: at certain moments he needs to believe that she loves him, at other moments he needs to believe that he is no longer in her power. The Terrorizer is perfectly aware of these needs, so she adjusts her conduct in such a way as to provide the kind of justification he is looking for, by increasing the strength of her manifestations of love at some times or the resoluteness of her rejections at others. Consequently, the situation can last for a very long time. Indeed, the couple may think that their story could last forever.

This is obviously their last illusion, for they have sufficient evidence for thinking that their story will not last forever. They are not the only persons entrapped in such a situation, and they know that sooner or later one of them will escape from it. If they believe that their story will last forever, it is because they desire that it will, however strange this may seem. The Terrorizer desires this because her influence on the Terrorized satisfies her desire or drive to dominate. But the Terrorized also desires it, in spite of the fact that he is the victim. The Terrorized resembles a smoker who desires a cigarette even if he does not want to desire it. Or he may have genuinely contradictory beliefs, which block him in some sort of cognitive paralysis. Only when the forms of self-deception produced by this contradiction lose their force, can the Terrorized finally free himself from the spell that holds him prisoner.

5

When love goes away

Il est impossible d'aimer une seconde fois ce qu'on a véritablement cessé d'aimer.

F. DE LA ROCHEFOUCAULD[1]

5.1 The end of love

Love is not eternal. When two persons love each other, their love develops within a limited interval of time, then it expires. In the most tragic cases, as in the case of Romeo and Juliet, the end of love is determined by external forces. But, generally, lovers do not die because they have broken some rule dictated by their families. In most cases, they live long enough to see the end of their love. Their feelings simply decrease until they no longer exist.

As noted in Section 1.2, love does not depend on the will. When one falls out of love, there is nothing one can do about it. One cannot simply decide to stay in love. Similarly, the other person's love cannot disappear at will simply because one's love is gone. This is why the end of one's love can be very painful for the other person. The pain may persist for long time, as in this song:

> Si las cosas que uno quiere
> se pudieran alcanzar;
> tú me quisieras lo mismo
> que veinte años atrás.
> Con qué tristeza miramos
> un amor que se nos va.
> Es un pedazo del alma
> que se arranca sin piedad.[2]

G. ARAMBURU, *Veinte años*

Many songs describe this. The affliction caused by the realization that one's feeling is no longer requited is a source of sadness, which may come in many forms, bitter sadness, desperate sadness, mournful sadness, lacerating sadness and so on. Psychologists often compare the separation from the beloved with the experience of bereavement, because in both cases one suffers the loss of a person perceived as being part of one's life. And the disvalue of loss stands to the emotional reaction of sadness as injustice to indignation, danger to fear.

However, separation from the beloved is not particularly interesting from an epistemological point of view. Certainly, when one is left by a person but is still in love with that person, at the beginning one will be reluctant to accept the change, so one may easily fall into wishful thinking. In such a situation, it is natural to think that perhaps the other is confused, that the other's words are not to be taken literally, that the other is going through a difficult period and so on. But as time passes and the facts become increasingly evident, these unjustified beliefs lose force, so one acknowledges the end of love and falls into a state of sadness that does not involve specific cognitive mistakes.

We are more interested in the person who falls out of love. If one realizes that one's love has ended, and that it cannot be replaced by friendship or conjugal love, then one may suffer as well. Especially if one still cares deeply for the other. In this case, one may feel unable to preserve one's love, and at the same time guilty about being the origin of the unhappiness of the other person. It may even happen that two persons stop loving each other, but that both of them feel pain over the end of their love. After all, it is sad to realize that such a beautiful thing is lost forever and will never come back.

In this chapter, we shall consider some typical situations in which one stops loving a person, and we shall focus on some forms of self-deception that one may experience in such situations. Since love comes in degrees, as noted in Section 1.2, the process that leads to the extinction of love is a gradual one. Schematically, this decrease can be divided into three phases, which we will call *the three phases of separation*. In the first phase, one starts questioning one's relationship with a person, even though most of the time one is convinced that one loves that person. In the second phase, one has opposite inclinations and does not really know whether one loves that person: some dispositions suggest that one is still in love, while others suggest the contrary. In the third phase, one knows that one no longer loves that person, or at least one's conviction that one no longer loves that person is stronger than one's inclination to believe that one still loves that person. Obviously, the duration and the significance of each of these three phases may vary from case to case. However, the tripartition is useful in order to identify the forms of self-deception that characterize each of them. In each of the three cases, one may have a wrong perception of one's feelings, and prolong unnecessarily the process of separation from the other person.

5.2 The sunk costs fallacy

Concorde was a supersonic jet airliner jointly developed by Aérospatiale and the British Aircraft Corporation under an Anglo-French treaty. First flown in 1969, Concorde entered service in 1976 and continued flying until 2003. Alongside the various factors that led to its retirement, which include some structural issues and one fatal accident that occurred in 2000, the main motivation was its huge costs. At some point it became clear that the two airlines involved, Air France and British

Airways, could make more profit using subsonic jet airliners. Obviously, when France and Great Britain first decided to invest in this project, the financial resources that they assigned to it were relatively limited. But during development the costs gradually and inevitably increased, while handling technical problems that arose due to its high speed and overheating. At each step, both governments decided to keep investing, because they had already spent a lot of money on the project. Thus, they ended up spending an enormous amount of money, much more than they had originally planned. Probably, if France and Great Britain had known from the beginning how much the Concorde was going to cost, they would have never decided to finance it.

The history of Concorde illustrates a common mistake that is easily described in economic terms. Economists generally assume that decisions should not be influenced by sunk costs, that is, by costs that have already been incurred and cannot be recovered. Suppose that you buy a ticket for a show, but later find out that it is a show you do not want to see. Should you go to the show? The most rational decision is not to go. Paying the ticket and using your time to do something else is better than paying the ticket and watching a show that you do not like, for in the second case you suffer twice. In either case, the price of the ticket has already been paid, so it should not be taken into account. Your decision should be based on whether you want to see the show, regardless of the price you have already paid, just as if the show were free. Nonetheless, people often reason differently. Since I spent the money – they think – I ought to go to the show. This is precisely what happened in the history of Concorde. At each stage of the development of the project, what influenced the decision to keep spending was the large amount of money that had already been spent earlier.

Lovers tend to reason in similar ways when they deliberate over their emotional investments. In the first phase of separation, typically when one considers the possibility of leaving a person, one may commit the *sunk costs fallacy*. It may happen that, in spite of the fact that the reasons for leaving that person are becoming increasingly evident, one thinks that, since one has invested a lot in that person over the previous months or years, it is worth making a further effort and preserve the relationship instead of losing everything. In such a case, one's policy may have disastrous effects, because the relationship may gradually change and become something that one would have never accepted at the beginning. In other words, one may end up watching many shows that one does not like at all.

The sunk costs fallacy may induce a person to drag out a relationship beyond the limits of reasonableness, for the will to preserve the emotional investment may prevail over the awareness of the problems that affect the relationship. This conservative attitude may lead to extreme and morbid forms of symbiosis or parasitism, where one ends up tolerating things that one would never tolerate otherwise, such as problems of money, alcohol, drug addiction or even violence.

5.3 The sweet lemons fallacy

Another mistake that lovers tend to commit when they deliberate about the future of their relationships resembles the sunk costs fallacy in at least two respects: it has a pretty obvious economic analogue, and it involves a conservative attitude that can harm the lovers themselves. This mistake may be regarded as a specific exemplification of a general fact, namely, that people tend to overvalue what they have.

Some economists have observed that ownership may foster irrational behaviour. When one owns a good, one is naturally inclined to overestimate its value. Or at least, the price for which one would be willing to sell the good is higher than its actual value. For example, if you are about to sell your house, you may easily think that it is worth 300,000 euros, while nobody would buy it for more than 250,000 euros. This depends on various psychological factors. First, you are historically linked to your house, so you associate it with some meaningful events in your past: you have spent many cheerful moments in its kitchen, your son took his first steps in its living room and so on. Second, you focus on what you may lose, rather than on what you may gain: you think that you will miss the sight of the hills from your desk, instead of imagining the house that you could buy if you had the 250,000 euros. Third, you take for granted that other people will see the transaction from the same perspective as you do: you expect the buyer of your house to appreciate the elegant design of its windows, whereas she is more likely to notice that the wall of its bedroom is too small for her closet.[3]

Lovers often reason like owners when they experience moments of hesitation or uncertainty during the first or the second phase of separation. When one considers the possibility of leaving a person, one may commit the *sweet lemons fallacy*, that is, one may be apt to overestimate the value of that person due to psychological factors of the kind considered. Of course, when we talk about the value of a person, the term 'value' does not have the same meaning that it has when we talk about the value of a house. The value of a person cannot be measured against a single objective standard. However, it is plausible to allow that there is an interesting analogy between the two uses of the term. In both cases, the overvaluation crucially depends on the time and energy one has invested in something, which somehow becomes part of one's life.[4]

It is easy to see that one may overestimate the value of one's beloved in the same way in which one may overestimate the value of one's house. First, one tends to regard some shared past experiences as meaningful: having painted the house together, having travelled together and so on. Second, one focuses on what one may lose, rather than on what one may gain: one thinks about missing specific qualities of one's beloved, instead of imagining qualities of another person one might meet. Third, one takes for granted that other people will evaluate one's beloved in the same way, appreciating the positive features that one appreciates, and ignoring the negative features that one ignores.[5]

The sweet lemons fallacy, like the sunk costs fallacy, may induce a person to extend the duration of a relationship beyond what is reasonable, for his or her belief in the value of the other person may prevail over the problems that affect the relationship. As a matter of fact, the two fallacies may easily coexist. The desire to preserve one's emotional investment and the belief in the value of the other person often go together.

Two final notes. The first is that, when we say that one may overestimate the value of one's beloved because one regards some shared past experiences as meaningful, we do not want to deny that one's beloved can have value just in virtue of such experiences. As some philosophers have observed, the historical connection between the lover and the beloved plays a crucial role in the lover's evaluation of the beloved. But even assuming that the value that the beloved has for the lover depends at least in part on some 'historical properties' of the beloved, that is, on some properties of the beloved that concern past interaction with the lover, the lover may still give too much weight to those properties, or be influenced by other historical properties that do not make the beloved valuable. In other words, one may be wrong about the significance of some historical properties of one's beloved, just as one may be wrong about the significance of any other property of one's beloved.[6]

The second note concerns the degree of generality of the sweet lemons fallacy. We have said that this fallacy may occur in the first or in the second phase of separation. But nothing prevents it from occurring in circumstances in which lovers have no hesitation or uncertainty about their relationships. It is not even essential that *lovers* are involved. Since it is a general fact that people tend to overvalue what they have, it is plausible to expect that the sweet lemons fallacy can also occur without love, in other kinds of personal relationships. For example, a wife may overestimate the value of her husband even if she does not love him.

5.4 Inertia and uncertainty

The second phase of separation is that in which one has opposite inclinations towards a person. On the one hand, one is aware of some facts that may suggest that one still loves that person. On the other hand, one is aware of other facts that may suggest that one does not love that person anymore. Since the evidence of the first kind is neither significantly stronger nor significantly weaker than the evidence of the second kind, one does not know whether one loves that person. This phase is a necessary step in the process that leads to the extinction of one's love, given that the process tends to be gradual.

Suppose that you are on the top of a mountain and you start walking down along a path that descends through a forest and leads to a flat plain. At the beginning of the walk you can see clearly that you are still on the mountain. Similarly, at the end of the walk you can see clearly that you are on the plain. But during the walk you will reach a point where, due to the limitations of the visual field and to the continuous changes of inclination, you are unable to see whether or not you are still on the mountain.

When one goes through this period of uncertainty, one may easily be affected by some form of *inertia*. That is, one may be reluctant to accept that one does not know whether one is in love, and think instead that one is still in love, simply because this is the way things have been up to that moment. Inertia is a psychological force that constantly shapes our way of perceiving reality. If until now things have been a certain way, it is natural to assume that they are still that way, unless some clear negative evidence appears. Therefore, inertia may induce one to misrepresent one's condition. That is, one may believe that one's love for a person is still there – or even believe that one knows that one's love for that person is still there – even though one does not know whether one loves that person.

5.5 Desamor

The third phase of separation is that in which one has gone through the period of uncertainty that characterizes the second phase, and is convinced that one no longer loves a person. In this phase, one can experience a state that is very interesting from an epistemological point of view, and quite dramatic from the psychological point of view. We call it by its Spanish name, *desamor*. Pablo Neruda describes very clearly what one feels when one is in this state:

> Ya no la quiero, es cierto, pero cuánto la quise.
>
> Mi voz buscaba el viento para tocar su oído.
>
> De otro. Será de otro. Como antes de mis besos.
>
> Su voz, su cuerpo claro. Sus ojos infinitos.
>
> Ya no la quiero, es cierto, pero tal vez la quiero.
>
> Est tan corto el amor, y es tan largo el olvido.
>
> Porque en noches como ésta la tuve entre mis brazos,
>
> mi alma no se contenta con haberla perdido.[7]
>
> P. NERUDA, *Veinte poemas de amor y*
> *una canción desesperada*

When one feels desamor, one experiences the sensation expressed in these verses. In some moments, one is inclined to doubt that one's love for the other person has ended, and one may also 'feel' that love. In those moments one is apt to behave like a lover. For example, it is possible that one does not sleep well, that one is still sexually attracted to that person or that one's conduct is anomalous in some respects. But in spite of these sporadic signs of worry and doubt, one clearly does not have sufficiently strong love dispositions towards that person, and one knows it.

Note that desamor as we understand it is a specific way of undergoing the end of a love story. Not every love story, when it ends, gives rise to desamor. In many cases, a love story ends with pain, anger, guilt, but not with desamor. It may be the case that some persons, but not others, are susceptible to desamor. Or it may happen that the same person suffers desamor only at certain moments of his or her life but not in others. So, desamor is a state that can occur, but does not necessarily occur, at the end of a love story.

Note also that desamor significantly differs from the states described in Sections 5.2–5.4. When one commits the sunk costs fallacy or the sweet lemons fallacy, one decides to make an effort to preserve one's love, because one hopes that the final result will reward that effort. In the case of desamor, on the other hand, one has no hope, although one may still desire what one has lost.

One does not fight for one's love, because one knows that there is nothing to fight for. Similarly, when one goes through a period of uncertainty and has opposite inclinations towards a person, one is in a condition in which one does not know whether one loves that person. In the case of desamor, on the other hand, one knows that nothing can bring one's love back, because one has sufficient evidence for believing that the story has ended.

Now we shall describe desamor from an epistemological point of view. Let Pablo and his muse be our two characters. Although Pablo is no longer in love with his muse, at certain moments he is inclined to doubt this fact. At those moments, Pablo is suspended in an emotional interlude in which he does not know what to think about his own feelings. The cause of this suspension is that, at those moments, Pablo would like to love his muse. The love between Pablo and his muse made him happy. So if that love still existed, he would be happy, and obviously he desires to be happy. Moreover, the love between Pablo and his muse made her happy. So if that love still existed, she would be happy, and he desires that she be happy, assuming that he cares about her. Since Pablo would like to love his muse, he is inclined to doubt what he knows, namely, that he no longer loves her.

From the description just provided it turns out that Pablo is affected by a peculiar form of wishful thinking. Although Pablo knows that he no longer loves his muse, there are moments when he believes that he does not know this, because at those moments he would like to love her. Unlike the cases of wishful thinking considered so far, in this case the unjustified belief caused by desire is a second-order belief, because it is about a mental state of the very same person who has the belief. In other words, it is as if Pablo did not want to know what he knows, namely, that he no longer loves his muse, because that fact is unpleasant for him.

As usually happens in cases of wishful thinking, Pablo's unjustified belief – the belief that he does not know that he no longer loves his muse – is not entirely devoid of positive evidence. In fact, Pablo can see that sometimes he is inclined to behave like a lover, and such inclinations may induce him to think that it is not true that he no longer loves his muse. As noted in Section 1.3, truth is necessary for knowledge, so if it is not true that Pablo no longer loves his muse, then Pablo does not know that he no longer loves his muse. However, the negative evidence is considerably stronger, given that most of the time, and in most respects, Pablo does not behave like a lover. Thus Pablo is not justified in believing that he does not know that he no longer loves his muse, and is in fact justified in believing that he knows that he no longer loves his muse. Again, if sometimes Pablo believes that he does not know that he no longer loves his muse, it is because at those moments he desires it.

The mistake just outlined is just one form of self-deception that may affect a person who stops loving another person. Since desamor is a state that can occur, but does not necessarily occur, towards the end of a love story, other forms of self-deception are possible. For example, one may reason like the fox and think instead that the love story that is just ending was not so wonderful as one imagined, so as to alleviate one's sense of loss. It may also happen that a person stops loving another person without falling into any kind of self-deception. One may simply accept that one's love for someone is dead, and that it cannot be replaced by a different form of relationship that is equally intense or rewarding.

To conclude, we shall consider the case in which desamor involves not only one person who stops loving another person, but two persons who stop loving each other. When two lovers realize that their love is gone, they may both experience desamor. In this case, the effects of self-deception may be even more insidious, for the unjustified beliefs of each of the two lovers foster the unjustified beliefs of the other. Each lover will be reluctant to recognize his or her own lack of love, and this will induce the other to do the same. Usually, in a situation of this kind the two lovers indulge in long conversations about themselves or their relationship, seeking relief in the memories of their shared past, but in so doing they simply prolong the emotional interlude in which they are suspended. Due to the confusion generated by the combined effect of their wishful thinking, their conversations might last forever without leading anywhere.

Kiko: Do you remember how much we loved each other? A love like this cannot disappear.

Alex: Of course I remember. But now it's different, you know that it is. Maybe our love will never end. Such a beautiful thing cannot end. But we have to face facts. We must give ourselves the opportunity to start a new life, we cannot keep living in the past.

Kiko: Don't say that! I hate you! I don't want anyone else.

Alex: This is what you think right now. I think the same. If only it were true. Perhaps it is true. What has happened to us? Maybe if we try …

Kiko: You really mean that? Yes, let's try again! There is nothing stronger than love! Everything depends on us, just on us.

Alex: Yes honey. Let's try and love each other as much as we can.

Kiko: That would be wonderful! Don't you agree? We could live again those wonderful moments. Though … it's sad. Thinking what we were … No, it doesn't make any sense! It's impossible. You know what happened last time. You are right, it is sad but we must face facts.

Alex: You want to give up? I love you. I feel it, here in my heart. Forget about what I just said. I was confused. Maybe I had some doubts, but now I know it.

Kiko: You say that only because you feel pity. Not only for me. You feel pity of both of us, for our love. You would like to love me, I know, but that is not going to happen. We must be strong. For our own good.

Alex: Now it's you who doesn't want to give me another chance. Don't give up! If we feel this way, it is for a reason.

Kiko: We only feel sorrow for what no longer exists ... I don't know ...

Alex: Maybe we are just confused ...

Kiko: No. We tried already, you know it. This time it is over. But I will always love you.

Alex: But ... I ... you ...

Kiko: No ... we ...

Etc, etc, etc.

6

FAQ

It was the passions about whose origin we deceived ourselves
that tyrannized most strongly over us.
O. WILDE, *THE PICTURE OF DORIAN GRAY*

In this last chapter, we address some questions that might easily cross the reader's mind. Each of these questions has actually been asked more than once during interviews and presentations of our works in Italian and Spanish, or raised in comments to previous versions of the present book. Even though the answers that we provide are implicitly contained in what we have already said in the previous chapters, it may be helpful to state them explicitly in order to avoid misunderstandings.

1. *Are you suggesting that one should not fall in love?*

No. Love is part of life, and we do not recommend abstention from it. It is not even clear that such a recommendation would make sense, given that love is not subject to the will. Falling in love, or not falling in love, is not exactly the kind of thing that one can decide after reading a philosophy book. Our investigation aims to shed some light on how people reason when they are in love, without implying anything about what they should or should not do. Here is an analogy. Behavioural economics studies the effects of emotional, cultural and social factors on the economic decisions of individuals and institutions. Empirical evidence suggests that people tend to make irrational choices when they buy clothes, cars or houses, and in some cases it is possible to identify patterns of fallacious reasoning that prove extremely persistent, deep-rooted and widespread. Yet anyone would agree that, when behavioural economists describe such patterns, it is not their intention to suggest that one should not make economic transactions. They take for granted that people buy clothes, cars or houses, and that there is nothing intrinsically wrong in doing such things. Our study of the fallacies of love is similar in this respect. We take for granted that people fall in love, and that there is nothing intrinsically wrong in doing it.

2. *Still you seem to imply that there is something wrong in unjustified love beliefs. What's wrong with them? After all, they may have positive consequences.*

The obvious answer to this question is that *there is* something wrong in unjustified love beliefs, namely, that they are unjustified. Of course, in many cases unjustified love beliefs have positive consequences. If lovers did not deceive themselves, they would lack the determination and the perseverance that are needed to get many things that they actually value. Imagine that Kiko unjustifiedly believes that Alex is the most handsome guy in the school, and that, as a consequence of this belief, she persistently pursues Alex for a year and flatters him with her attentions. In this case, it may happen that Alex ends up falling in love with Kiko and makes her happy. If it happens, then, all things considered, Kiko's unjustified belief is good for Kiko. The point, however, is that having positive effects does not prevent Kiko's belief from being unjustified. This is a general point that holds for any belief and has nothing to do with love. For example, if Kiko believes that she will get a raise if she works hard, and as a consequence of this belief she works hard and achieves certain results, it may happen that those results are beneficial for her in the long run. But this does not prevent Kiko's belief from being unjustified. Our work focuses on the normative dimension of justification, it is not concerned with the consequences of beliefs.

3. *What is the difference between love and sex? It seems that the dispositions you describe as characteristic of love also*

occur in passionate sexual relationships which people do
not usually classify as love.

This is a tricky question because most of the time, when
people draw a line between love and sex, they tend to use
the word 'love' in ways that are wider or looser than ours.
If we restrict the use of 'love' to romantic love and leave
aside conjugal love and other forms of affection that are
largely independent of sex, it is certainly true that love
relationships and passionate sexual relationships have
much in common: they involve essentially the same kinds
of dispositions. However, the intensity of some of these
dispositions is typically lower in relationships that are
predominantly sexual. For example, a sexual liaison very
often does not involve a strong and constant desire to
spend time together before or after having sex (at dinner,
in bed and so on). Such a desire is distinctive of love, or so
is commonly perceived. The same goes for the tendency
to behave irrationally when the other person is absent, or
even for the disposition to have certain bodily reactions.
So the difference between love and sex as we understand
it – assuming that there is such a difference – is ultimately
a matter of degree in certain characteristic dispositions.
Perhaps there is a bit of love in every passionate sexual
relationship.

4. *Do homosexual love and heterosexual love differ from an epistemological point of view?*

As far as we can see, there is no reason to think they do. Of course, we cannot rule out such differences *a priori*, and there is no point in speculating about statistics that we don't have. But in any case, it does not really matter for our purposes. As explained in Section 1.5, our goal is to identify and describe some characteristic cognitive mistakes, so we are interested in the mistakes themselves, rather than in who commits them.

5. *What about polyamory? In your discussion of the Divided Lover you seem to suggest that loving two or more persons implies falling into some form of self-deception. Isn't this but a sophisticated way of expressing an old bias in favour of monogamy?*

We have no bias in favour of monogamy, or against polyamory. Our background hypothesis that love is a dispositional state is entirely neutral with respect to the distinction between monogamous and non-monogamous relations or inclinations: just as one can have love dispositions towards a single person, one can have love dispositions towards two or more persons. It is the presence of love dispositions that opens the door to self-deception, rather than the number of persons involved. Accordingly, polyamory does not imply self-deception more than monogamy does. Just as one can love a single person with or without self-deception, one can love two or more persons with or without self-deception. The fallacy of the Divided Lover is a specific case of self-deception, which requires the subject to love at least two persons: to commit this fallacy, one must be involved in a non-monogamous relation. But this does not mean that whenever one is involved in a non-monogamous relation one commits the fallacy of the Divided Lover, or deceives oneself in some other way.

6. *Can we really distinguish romantic love from conjugal love?*

Yes, we can. Assuming that it makes sense to talk about conjugal love as a specific dispositional state that does not reduce to friendship or other kinds of affection, this state clearly differs from romantic love, at least in its paradigmatic manifestations. Conjugal love essentially involves caring. It is similar to friendship in that it develops gradually – rather than suddenly and unexpectedly – from a series of shared experiences. Another difference is that conjugal love need not involve the disposition to have repeated and prolonged sexual contact with the beloved. Moreover, conjugal love usually does not involve the disposition to do crazy things, at least not the kind of crazy things that lovers do. In this sense, it is less passionate than romantic love, and generally more rational and sensitive to means-ends considerations. For example, if one has money issues and barely gets to the end of the month, one will not spend half of the salary for a beautiful yet useless present for one's partner.

In another sense, though, conjugal love is passionate in its own way, as it involves a disposition to sacrifice one's interests for the sake of the other. Conjugal love can make you risk your life to save the other's life, even though you are unwilling to spend half of your salary on a useless present. This disposition to make sacrifices, together with the kind of attachment that characterizes long-term relationships, distinguishes a union based on conjugal love from a marriage of convenience or a similar form of shared life. So, conjugal love can be present in or absent from a couple, just like romantic love, and can increase or decrease with time.

7. *Isn't romantic love just a social construction?*

There certainly is a plausible sense in which romantic love is a social construction. As several historians and philosophers have observed, the stereotypes that are most commonly associated with love are cultural products created by a tradition of European intellectuals with their poems, novels and piano sonatas. It is important to understand, however, that our epistemological analysis of love beliefs is consistent with this observation.

The manifestations of love dispositions may change from culture to culture. For example, sexual inclinations may have different expressions in ancient Greece, medieval Japan or contemporary Sweden. The same goes for the tendency to do crazy things. Perhaps the only invariant effect of love, which depends on specific physical and psychological traits, is the one related to bodily reactions. But variation in the manifestations of love dispositions does not amount to variation in the kinds of dispositions involved. In particular, as explained in Section 1.6, it is reasonable to conjecture that there is a core of cognitive propensities that are universal.

We believe that, although the content of the unjustified beliefs that lovers have may be culturally determined to some extent, the disposition to have this kind of beliefs is not culturally determined. An example that illustrates this distinction is the case of the Princess discussed in Section 4.3. If a person desires to marry Prince Charming because she grew up with Cinderella and other fairy tales, and this desire induces her to believe that Prince Charming exists, she has an unjustified belief whose content is culturally determined. If she had grown up in a different environment, she would have different desires and beliefs. However, the tendency to believe what she desires, which is the psychological mechanism that generates her unjustified belief, is not itself a cultural product. Even if she had grown up in a different environment, with different ideals, probably the relation between her desires and her beliefs would be exactly the same.

8. *Is your book intended to deconstruct the mythology of love?*

Surely this was not our aim when we started thinking about the fallacies of love. Nevertheless, as some readers have pointed out, our epistemological analysis of love beliefs has an undeniable deconstructive power. Once one realizes that lovers tend to fall into the same kind of misconceptions, one naturally distances oneself from those misconceptions and regards them as myths. The case of the Princess is again an interesting example in this respect: Prince Charming is nothing but a myth.

Independently of the specific cognitive mistakes discussed in the previous chapters, our work questions the idealized conception of love according to which being in love is always good. In our answer to question 1 we said that there is nothing intrinsically wrong with falling in love. Now we can add that there is nothing intrinsically right. Love is what it is, whether it is good or bad depends on how people experience it. The conception of love as always psychologically 'positive' is simply ungrounded.

9. *Are the cognitive mistakes exclusive of love?*

No. The same mistakes can occur in any situation in which emotions affect the ability to think clearly. As a matter of fact, some of the fallacies that we describe in the book reveal very general psychological mechanisms. One telling example is wishful thinking, which occurs in a great variety of contexts in the forms illustrated in Sections 3.2 and 3.3. Parents usually tend to give excessive weight to the qualities of their children and are often unable to see their defects, so they behave exactly like lovers in this respect. The same kind of misperception can easily be triggered by other kinds of interpersonal relations due to friendship, ideology or religion. Other examples are the sunk costs fallacy and the sweet lemons fallacy. As explained in Sections 5.2 and 5.3, these two fallacies have obvious economic analogues, so they are not exclusive to love. In fact, we regard this lack of exclusivity of the fallacies of love as one of the most interesting aspects of our investigation. We believe that the study of the fallacies of love can shed light on some deep psychological tendencies that generate irrational beliefs in highly emotional situations and could ideally be described at a higher level of generality.

10. *Will I commit fewer mistakes after reading your book?*

No. As explained in Section 1.6, knowing a certain cognitive mistake does not prevent one from making that mistake. For example, perceptual illusions do not disappear when they are revealed. The Muller-Lyer illusion, which makes you believe that one arrow is longer than other, does not disappear when you realize that the two arrows have the same length, not even if you learn the perceptual mechanism that produces the illusion. A scientist who knows everything about optical illusions is still susceptible to optical illusions. The same goes for the fallacies of love. Knowing the fallacies of love does not prevent you from committing them.

This is not to say that our book is entirely useless. The knowledge of the fallacies of love can help to limit their negative effects if combined with other motivational factors, such as the memory of past suffering, the help of a good friend or some sessions of psychotherapy. For example, reading Section 4.5 certainly will not make you immune to emotional terrorism. The motivational impact of a few pages is certainly not comparable to that of a real experience of emotional terrorism. But if you have suffered an episode of emotional terrorism and you want to avoid falling into the same trap again, reading Section 4.5 may be of some help. After all, knowing a cognitive mistake is better than not knowing it.

NOTES

Chapter 1

1 Love, impossible to define.

2 Recent works on the neurophysiology of love include Fisher (2004) and Young and Alexander (2014).

3 This tendency does not rule out that love, just as other passions, can have an epistemic value of some kind, or can be associated with virtuous cognitive processes. Several philosophers, such as Brady (2013), have argued that emotions play an important epistemic role. More generally, we are not assuming that passions always hinder cognitive processes.

4 Naar (2018) suggests that the hypothesis that love is a dispositional state is justified on the basis of general reasons.

5 Or at least, this is the traditional view. We do not rule out the possibility that empirical evidence shows that, in certain circumstances, love dispositions can be modified using chemical or psychological techniques.

6 The first definition is suggested in Taylor (1976), Newton-Smith (1989), Soble (1990), LaFollette (1996), Frankfurt (1999) and White (2001). The second, which goes back to Aristotle, is advocated in Solomon (1981), Scruton (1986), Nozick (1989), Fisher (1990) and Delaney (1996). The third is developed in different ways in Velleman (1999) and in Kolodny (2003).

7 The latter issue is addressed, among other works, in Goldie (2010), Smuts (2014), Naar (forthcoming), Brogaard (2015) and Brogaard (2018).

8 As Naar (2013) observes, p. 355, one of the merits of the hypothesis that love is a dispositional state is precisely that it explains the apparent epistemic opacity of love.

9 Although the term 'fallacy' is traditionally used to refer to a bad argument that appears good, it can also be used to refer to the conclusion of such an argument, that is, to an unjustified belief that appears justified. Here we will talk about fallacies mainly in the second sense.

10 This is particularly clear when a stereotype is heavily gender-biased, because the demystifying effects works against gender inequality, as suggested in Pérez Sedeño (2018).

11 Note that this conjecture is consistent with different views of love. In particular, it is consistent with any naturalistic view of love, such as that suggested in Fisher (2004), and with any non-naturalistic view that grants some basic biological facts about love, such as that suggested in Jenkins (2017).

Chapter 2

1 The term was initially used in Jones (1908), and then adopted by Sigmund Freud.

2 This is one of the many versions of the fable, provided by Phaedrus.

3 Singer (2009) claims that love is essentially a matter of bestowing value on the beloved. Much of what we have said about the you–you fallacy and the virtue fallacy is consistent with this claim.

4 If the fox simply ceased to desire the grapes, or formed the positive desire not to eat them, he would make no mistake. We would have what Elster (1983) calls an 'adaptive preference', that is, a desire that has adapted to what is available.

5   I didn't love her when I met her, / Until one night she told me,
    resolute: / I'm already very tired of everything … and she left. / What
    does life, brother, have in store for us! / From that moment I started to
    love her.

Chapter 3

1   Perhaps the tale was true, but hardly likely / To one who was in
    command of his senses; / But it seemed easily possible to him, / Who
    had fallen into a worse mistake. / What a man sees, Love makes
    invisible / And Love reveals what is invisible. / This was believed; for
    the frail are apt / To give easy trust to things that please.

2   Jollimore (2011) contains some reflections on how the appreciation of
    the beloved's properties 'silences' a similar appreciation of the same
    properties in other persons, although – unlike the present work – it
    attributes a positive normative significance to this phenomenon.
    According to Jollimore, when one loves a person, one actively attends
    to the person's valuable properties in a way that coherently provides
    one with reasons to treat the person preferentially.

3   According to more specific versions of the commonplace, the price of
    the ring must satisfy certain constraints, such as bearing a certain ratio
    to the gross salary of the boyfriend.

Chapter 4

1   Love is being stupid together.

2   Catron (2017), pp. 93–117, provides a lucid and clear-headed analysis of
    the legacy of Cinderella in popular romantic films.

3 My dear lady, this is a list / Of the beauties my master has loved; / a list that I have put together; / Observe and read along with me. / In Italy six hundred and forty; / In Germany two hundred and thirty; / One hundred in France, in Turkey ninety-one; / But in Spain already one thousand and three. / Among these are country women, / Serving wenches, city girls, / There are countesses, baronesses, / Marchionesses, princesses. / And women of all ranks, / Of every shape, of all ages.

4 This unquenchable zest / that finds itself inside me, / every day more terribly / increasing, blazing higher / ... Time and absence, in vain, though / seek to extinguish it / for doubling in violence, / it is no longer a fire, but a volcano. / And I, suspended / I battle without shelter, / in the midst of a crater / between my tomb and my Inés. / ... Inés, soul of my soul, / my life's eternal goal, / a pearl concealed, without a shell, / deep beneath the ocean swell.

5 I just don't know. I'm going mad. One moment / she dotes on me, the next she turns against me. / She won't have me, or let me have Marcela, / and if I keep away, she finds at once / some trumped-up reason why she has to see me. / She is the dog in the manger / won't eat, nor let eat. / she's neither in, nor out.

6 Yes indeed, so little / that though I feel, I cannot comprehend / I feel your blows, can't comprehend your words / You're angry if I love you, or I don't. / If I forget, you write; if I remember, / you say I'm wrong; you'd have me understand you / and if I understand you, I'm a fool. / So give me life, or death; give me some quarter / some happy mean between these wild extremes.

Chapter 5

1 It is impossible to love a second time what we have really ceased to love.

2 If one could reach / the things one wants, / you would love me the same way / you loved me twenty years ago / With such sadness we

look / at a love that is gone. / It is a piece of soul / that is ripped out without pity.

3 Ariely (2008), pp. 127–38, illustrates this phenomenon and suggests a psychological explanation of the kind considered.

4 The name 'sweet lemons' comes from Elster (1983).

5 If you do not like the comparison between owning a house and being with someone, because you think that personal relationships have nothing to do with property, note that what really matters here is not owning the house, but simply being used to it. For example, people often tend to overvalue their home town in similar ways, even though it does not belong to them.

6 The historical connection between the lover and the beloved is considered in Whiting (1991), Delaney (1996), Kolodny (2003), Grau (2010).

7 I no longer love her, that's certain, but how I loved her. / My voice tried to find the wind to reach her. / Another's. She will be another's. As she was before my kisses. / Her voice, her shining body, her unfathomable eyes. / I no longer love her, that's certain, but perhaps I love her. / Love is so short, forgetting is so long. / Since, on nights like this one I held her in my arms, / my soul is not content to have lost her.

BIBLIOGRAPHY

Ariely, D. (2008), *Predictably Irrational*. HarperCollins.

Brady, M. S. (2013), *Emotional Insight*, Oxford University Press.

Brogaard, B. (2015), *On Romantic Love: Simple Truths about a Complex Emotion*. Oxford University Press.

Brogaard, B. (2018), 'Romantic love for a reason'. In *Oxford Handbook of Philosophy of Love*, edited by C. Grau and A. Smuts. Oxford University Press.

Catron, M. L. (2017), *How to Fall in Love with Anyone*. Simon and Schuster.

Delaney, N. (1996), 'Romantic Love and Loving Commitment: Articulating a Modern Ideal'. *American Philosophical Quarterly* 33: 375–405.

Elster, J. (1983), *Sour Grapes*. Cambridge University Press.

Elster, J. (1999), *Alchemies of the Mind: Rationality and the Emotions*. Cambridge University Press.

Fisher, H. (2004), *Why We Love: The Nature and Chemistry of Romantic Love*. Henrio Holt .

Fisher, M. (1990), *Personal Love*. Duckworth.

Frankfurt, H. (1999), 'Necessity, Volition, and Love'. In *Autonomy, Necessity, and Love*, 129–41. Cambridge University Press.

Goldie, P. (2010), 'Love for a Reason'. *Emotion Review* 2: 61–7.

Grau, C. (2010), 'Love and History'. *Southern Journal of Philosophy* 48: 246–71.

Jenkins, C. (2017), *What Love Is and What It Could Be*. Basic Books.

Jollimore, T. (2011), *Love's Vision*. Princeton University Press.

Jones, E. (1908), 'Rationalization in Everyday Life'. *Journal of Abnormal Psychology* 3: 161–9.

Kolodny, N. (2003), 'Love as Valuing a Relationship'. *Philosophical Review* 112: 135–89.

LaFollette, H. (1996), *Personal Relationships: Love, Identity, and Morality*. Blackwell Press.

Naar, H. (2013), 'A Dispositional Theory of Love'. *Pacific Philosophical Quarterly* 94: 342–57.

Naar, N. (2018), 'Love as a Disposition', in *Oxford Handbook of Philosophy of Love*, edited by C. Grau and A. Smuts. Oxford University Press.

Naar, N. (forthcoming), 'The Possibility of Fitting Love: Irreplaceability and Selectivity', *Synthese*.

Newton-Smith, W. (1989), 'A Conceptual Investigation of Love', in *Eros, Agape, and Philia: Readings in the Philosophy of Love*, edited by A. Soble, 199–217. Paragon House.

Nozick, R. (1989), 'The Examined Life: Philosophical Meditations', in *Love's Bond*, 68–86. Simon and Schuster.

Pérez Sedeño, E. (2018), 'Nota sobre *Del Amor y otros engaños*', *Critica*.

Scruton, R. (1986), *Sexual Desire: A Moral Philosophy of the Erotic*. Free Press.

Singer, I. (2009), *Philosophy of Love: A Partial Summing-up*. MIT Press.

Smuts, A. (2014), 'Normative Reasons for Love'. *Philosophy Compass* 9, no. 8: 507–26.

Soble, A. (1990), *The Structure of Love*. Yale University Press.

Solomon, R. C. (1981), *Love: Emotion, Myth, and Metaphor*. Anchor Press.

Taylor, G. (1976), 'Love', *Proceedings of the Aristotelian Society* 76: 147–64

Velleman, J. D. (1999), 'Love as a Moral Emotion', *Ethics*, 109: 338–74.

White, R. J. (2001), *Love's Philosophy*. Rowman and Littlefield.

Whiting, J. E. (1991), 'Impersonal Friend', *Monist*, 74: 3–29.

Young, L., and B. Alexander (2014), *The Chemistry between Us: Love, Sex and the Science of Attraction*. Penguin Books.

INDEX

www.ingramcontent.com/pod-product-compliance
Ingram Content Group UK Ltd.
Pitfield, Milton Keynes, MK11 3LW, UK
UKHW020714280225
455688UK00012B/364